ESPRESSO

P9-DHB-128

ESPRESSO

ULTIMATE COFFEE

SECOND EDITION

Kenneth Davids

ST. MARTIN'S GRIFFIN

NEW YORK

ESPRESSO: ULTIMATE COFFEE, SECOND EDITION. Copyright © 1993, 2001 by Kenneth Davids. All rights reserved. Printed in the United States of America. No part of this book may be used or reproduced in any manner whatsoever without written permission except in the case of brief quotations embodied in critical articles or reviews. For information, address St. Martin's Press, 175 Fifth Avenue, New York, NY 10010.

www.stmartins.com

Production Editor: David Stanford Burr

Library of Congress Cataloging-in-Publication Data

Davids, Kenneth.

    Espresso : ultimate coffee / Kenneth Davids.—2nd ed.
        p.   cm.
    Includes index.
    ISBN 0-312-24666-8
     1. Espresso.   I. Title.
    TX817.C6 D37 2001
    641.3'373—dc21   00-045824

First St. Martin's Griffin Edition: May 2001

10 9 8 7 6 5 4 3 2 1

CONTENTS

PREFACE

ESPRESSO AND ME

Some years back I realized that espresso cuisine was definitely established in America when Dave's Coffee Shop in Oakland, California, situated across the street from two automobile dealers and next to a store selling floor coverings, put up a large sign indicating that it too, along with every other place in town, finally served "espresso" (spelled correctly, with an "s"), thus assuring that the nearby automobile salesmen and high school students, not to mention motorists on the long, dry run between caffès in downtown Oakland and Berkeley, need no longer be deprived of their cappuccino or caffè latte.

This is a book that attempts to demystify espresso in all of its varied incarnations: from the purist's short pull to the shopping mall cuisine of chocolate-almond caffè lattes. Espresso cuisine is mysterious not only because it is produced by large, complex machines that make locomotivelike noises, but also because it is a relatively new alternative coffee tradition to the American cuisine of medium-roasted, light-bodied filter coffee. And because it is a different tradition, it brings with it other culinary procedures, other institutions, other rituals.

In the following pages I've tried to respond to most of the questions that might be asked about espresso: questions about its technical aspects, its history, its mythology, its culture, and above all, how to do whatever you want to do with it at home. I've attempted to give clear and complete advice about all aspects of producing good home espresso cuisine, while adding enough espresso history, fact, and myth to bring the procedures to life.

The Espresso Generation

My own involvement with espresso, at least in what might be called a professional sense, goes back to the time in my life when I nursed a cranky old Cimbali espresso machine in a caffè I co-owned and managed in Berkeley, California. Subsequently I sold the caffè and wrote a book on coffee, which is now in its fifth edition: *Coffee: A Guide to Buying, Brewing, and Enjoying.* But espresso was not an afterthought in my personal coffee history. In fact, it started my coffee history. Since my experience is in many ways typical of my generation of coffee drinkers, it might be worth pursuing briefly.

Like many Americans who came of age in the early 1960s, I did not grow up drinking coffee. The only pressing choice I faced was whether to drink Pepsi or Coca-Cola. Coffee was sourish brown stuff drunk for unknown reasons by people over thirty, presumably while they occupied themselves with other peculiar middle-aged activities, like watching Ed Sullivan, listening to Frank Sinatra, and petting their cocker spaniels.

"Do You Like *Coffee?*"

The first inkling I had that there might be something worthwhile to the beverage was during my first college-student trip to Europe. While hitchhiking from France to Italy, I was picked up by a ruddy-faced Italian doctor. When we reached the Italian side of the border, he turned, squinted at me, drew himself up, and intoned grandly: "Do you like *coffee?*" The well-traveled reader will understand the length and sonorous authority of the vowels sounding in that question.

I responded that I wasn't sure. Whereupon the doctor literally skidded to a stop in front of the next espresso bar (actually the first espresso bar, since we had just entered Italy), strode up to the counter, ordered two espressos, dumped several spoonfuls of sugar in his, muddled them, and drank the results, all in about the time that it took me to follow him in from the car.

I didn't much care for that first dark little cup, but somewhere between Genoa and Florence I learned, like most Americans do, to order a cappuccino, and from there progressed and regressed through the rest of the carefully modulated drinks of the Italian espresso cuisine, from milky latte macchiato to the *corto* espresso, barely enough rich, heavy, creamy espresso to cover the bottom of a demitasse. Along the way I learned to stand properly with one elbow on the bar, stare at the passing Fiats while downing my espresso drink in several swallows, then replace the cup on the saucer with the proper authoritative clack. Above all I learned to love the peculiar bittersweet richness of espresso drinks, which rings on one's taste-buds like a delicious dark bellclap, a sort of musical accompaniment to the lingering resonance of the caffeine.

On my return to the United States I discovered the Italian-American caffè, that more leisurely, spacious throwback to an Italy before the advent of the espresso bar, and began to drink my cappuccinos in places like the Caffè Reggio in Manhattan, the Caffè Mediterraneum in Berkeley, and the Caffè Trieste in San Francisco. Caffès became my true home. Because most of them were across the street from a bookstore, I had everything I needed in life clustered around my temporarily rented marbletop table: books, newspapers, espresso coffee, sympathetic friends, plus an occasional sandwich. I recall spending long, fruitless hours in towns with neither Italians nor caffès, driving around looking for a proper cappuccino and a proper place to drink it. When I taught at the University of Hawaii for a year, I ended up learning not only to make my own cappuccino but roast my own coffee as well, since in those years there was not a single dark-roasted coffee bean on the entire island of Oahu, aside from the ones I roasted myself in a frying pan in my tin-roofed bungalow in Kaneohe.

Given that history, it perhaps was inevitable that I would be drawn to opening my own caffè, which I eventually did, and writing, first a book about coffee generally, and then a book on espresso in particular.

Espresso Thanks

In the course of that writing I have run up an enormous collective debt to those involved in the art and business of coffee and espresso.

My thanks first to those individuals and businesses, particularly the Victoria Arduino company, the publishers of William Ukers' *All About Coffee,* and BE-MA Editrice, publishers of Ambrogio Fumagalli's *Macchine da Caffè,* or permitting me to make use of illustrations from their publications.

When I turn from businesses to individuals the list of those to whom I am indebted grows much longer. In fact, impossibly long. All I can do is name a few individuals whose input was particularly crucial in the making of the two editions of this book.

I would like to particularly thank Bob Barker, who read through the entire typescript of the first edition and made many valuable suggestions; collector Ambrogio Fumagalli of Milan; Christopher and John Cara of Thomas Cara, Ltd.; Don Holly and Ted Lingle of the Specialty Coffee Association of America; Sherri Miller of Miller & Associates; Kevin Knox of Allegro Coffee; the coffee cupper and pundit George Howell; Bruce Milletto of Bellissimo Coffee Education Group; Jim Reynolds of Peet's Coffee & Tea; Don Schoenholt of Gillies Coffee; Lindsey Bolger of Batdorf & Bronson; Carl Staub of Agtron; and I had better stop there or the publisher will be forced to add another signature to the book.

To those individuals I would add the numerous others who assisted me in the research for the several editions of *Coffee: A Guide to Buying, Brewing & Enjoying* and for *Home Coffee Roasting: Romance & Revival.*

I consulted several useful books during the course of assembling this one, in particular Ambrogio Fumagalli's *Macchine da Caffè;* Ian Bersten's *Coffee Floats, Tea Sinks;* Edward and Joan Bramah's *Coffee Makers, 300 Years of Art & Design;* Francesco and Riccardo Illy's *Coffee to Espresso;* the Italian version of Felipe Ferre's *Il Caffè;* Ralph Hattox's *Coffee and Coffeehouses, The Origins of a Social Beverage in the Medieval Near East;* the Italian Istituto Internazionale Assaggiatori Caffè's *Espresso Tasting;* Andrea Illy and R. Viani's *Espresso Coffee: The Chemistry of Quality;* and Mariarosa Schiaffino's *Le Ore del Caffè* and *Cioccolato & Cioccolatini.* Finally, the works of Michael Sivitz and William Ukers continue to be invaluable.

The notes and records of the ongoing saga of coffee and coffee culture recorded in *Tea and Coffee Trade Journal, Fresh Cup,* and other coffee industry magazines were constantly useful, as were the publications of the Specialty Coffee Association of America.

Finally, I am delighted to have an opportunity to thank my original editor, Annette Gooch, and my current editor, Keith Kahla; my agents, Richard Derus and Claudia Menza, and illustrator Michael Surles.

A concluding word of gratitude to those many professionals and enthusiasts in the United States, Italy, and Latin America whose insight has enriched and enlivened my view of espresso, even though I may have lost their cards or misplaced my scribbles on the backs of product literature. The achievements of this book are owing in great part to those who assisted me; the mistakes are mine alone.

1 ULTIMATE COFFEE

ESPRESSO DEFINITIONS

At the level at which we genuinely live life, every reader of this book will have a different definition of espresso. For some, that definition may be a long-developed acquaintance with the beverage, an accumulation of happy memories of caffès and tinkering with home machines, of frothed milk and *crema*. For others "espresso" may mean a single experience with a caffè latte taken at an outdoor espresso stand during a vacation, or a couple of cappuccinos drunk while on a trip to Italy. Like coffee itself, espresso is as much an experience caught up in the intimate textures of our lives as it is a beverage.

Yet even when we attempt to define espresso in more detached fashion, there still appear to be many overlapping definitions, rather than a single, all-inclusive one.

A TECHNICAL DEFINITION

A definition of espresso along technical lines is perhaps least ambiguous: Espresso is coffee brewed from beans roasted medium to dark brown, with the brewing accomplished by hot water forced (or "pressed") through a bed of finely ground, densely compacted coffee at a pressure of over 9 atmospheres, or nine times the normal pressure exerted by the earth's atmosphere. The resulting heavy-bodied, aromatic, bittersweet beverage is often combined with milk that has been heated and aerated by having steam run through it until the milk is hot and covered by a head of froth.

To extend the technical definition somewhat, we might say that espresso is an entire system of coffee production, a system that includes specific approaches to blending the coffee, to roasting it and grinding it, and that emphasizes freshness through grinding and brewing coffee a cup at a time on demand, rather than brewing a pot or urn at a time from pre-ground coffee and letting the result sit until it is served.

A HISTORICAL AND CULTURAL DEFINITION

Defining espresso culturally and historically is more problematic. The taste for a dark, heavy, intense coffee, sweetened and drunk out of little cups, is obviously much older than the espresso machine itself, and may stretch back as far as the first coffeehouses in Cairo, Egypt, established during the early fifteenth century. On the other hand, technology (and the imagery of technology) is also obviously an important element of espresso culture. Although all coffee making lends itself to technological tinkering, no other coffee culture has applied technology to coffee making with quite the passion as the Italians have to espresso. The word "espresso" itself suggests custom brewing, as in brewed *expressly* for you, as well as direct, rapid, nonstop, as in *express* train. Not only has technology been applied enthusiastically to the actual process of brewing espresso, but the imagery of technology, the idea of modernity and speed, also turns up as a major element in espresso's cultural symbolism. See the famous Victoria Arduino poster from the 1920s on page vii, for example.

So culturally and historically we have a paradox. On the one hand, espresso as a general taste in coffee drinking goes back to the very beginnings of coffee as a public beverage. On the other, Italian espresso culture has refined that taste through a technology that flaunts its modernity.

When we turn our attention to the United States, a historical and cultural definition of espresso might emphasize still another set of connotations. Rather than being associated with modernity and a dynamic urbanism, espresso in America has become identified with various alternative cultures, from Europeanized sophisticates nostalgically evoking tradition, to intellectual rebels attacking it.

ESPRESSO AS CUISINE

Espresso also can be defined as a kind of coffee *cuisine.* For example, mainstream American coffee cuisine emphasizes the bottomless cup: large, repeated servings of usually brisk-tasting, light-bodied coffees prepared by the filter method, often taken without milk or sweetener. Espresso cuisine, on the other hand, emphasizes smaller servings of heavier-bodied, richer coffee, brewed on demand rather than in batches, usually drunk sweetened, and often combined with frothed milk and other garnishes and flavorings.

In Italy the classic espresso cuisine emphasizes simplicity: perfect short pulls of espresso and a handful of exquisitely modulated combinations of coffee and milk. Predictably, in North America a more freewheeling, idiosyncratic, bigger approach has evolved. At one extreme the Seattle-style espresso cuisine rears its many-flavored head: wide open, innovative, the basic themes of espresso and milk exuberantly elaborated with flavored syrups, ice, a score of garnishes, and seemingly endless refinements involving the milk (1 percent, 2 percent, 4 percent, skim, soy, eggnog . . .). At the other is beatnik espresso, the original Italian-American cuisine, the espresso of storefront shops in old Italian neighborhoods and seedy artists' caffès. This cuisine resembles the classic Italian, but the coffee is darker, the servings are bigger, and the taste is rawer. Between the two are a few, very few, caffès that conscientiously pursue the classic Italian ideal. The Cuban tradition of southern Florida constitutes still another, though more regional, American espresso cuisine.

Finally, there is still another American cuisine, which I would like to dub *espresso manqué,* and which is all of the misinterpretations and misunderstandings of espresso being committed in the United States today thrown together, including watery, bitter, overextracted coffee, scalded milk, meringuelike heads of froth, all presented to the background flatulence of canned whipped cream being sprayed on top of the drink to distract us from the grim reality underneath.

A DEFINITION BY PLACE

Finally, espresso can be defined in terms of the places it has helped create and that helped create it: the caffès, cafés, coffeehouses, espresso bars, and espresso carts of the world. For espresso is a quintessentially public coffee. The technological sophistication of the espresso system only could have evolved in the context of public establishments with enough coffee drinkers to support the expense involved in maintaining such large and complex coffee-making equipment. Thus espresso and the espresso machine have come to constitute the spiritual and aesthetic heart of a variety of subtly different institutions, including the Italian-American caffè, the espresso bar, the American coffeehouse, and now the Seattle-style espresso cart and stand.

THE NICE VICE

I'm drawn to add still one more definition, something along contemporary sociological lines. For it appears that fancy coffees generally, and espresso cuisine in particular, have assumed a rather unique role in contemporary American life. It is a role that has led some commentators to characterize coffee (and caffeine) as the "nice vice" of the millennium, the one pleasantly consciousness-altering substance that has escaped (perhaps narrowly) from the censure heaped by a health-conscious establishment on alcohol, tobacco, and their various illegal alternatives. Certainly the current crop of college-age youth, a generation I find particularly attractive, has adopted coffee as a beverage and ritual of choice. Fifties-style coffeehouses are booming, and T-shirts and lapel buttons surface wherever younger people congregate, half seriously, half ironically celebrating coffee. "Espresso Yourself," says one; "Coffee Is God" proclaims another.

So is everything else, the Buddhist might reply, but for some of us a particularly good case can be made for our favorite drink.

A contemporary espresso cart, an increasingly familiar sight in North American shopping malls, downtown streets, and even gasoline stations.

ESPRESSO BREAK
THE ESPRESSO BAR SYSTEM

Delivery of a tiny, aromatic cup of espresso or a perfectly balanced cappuccino depends on an integrated brewing system, including machine, grinder, and accessories. The various elements of a complete commercial espresso system are illustrated on the next page.

The machine. The machine pictured here is a simple semi-automatic pump machine. The operator or *barista* dispenses ground coffee into a metal filter fixed inside a filter holder, clamps the filter and filter holder into the machine, and presses a button to start and stop the flow of brewing water through the coffee. For illustrated descriptions of other types of machines, including manual piston and fully automatic, see pages 24–34.

The *housing* (1) of the machine conceals a water reservoir, a pump to push the brewing water through the coffee, apparatus for heating and measuring the brewing water, and a boiler in which the water used to create steam for milk frothing is held and heated. The apparatuses that heat water for brewing and for making steam are separate, since the ideal water temperature for brewing is somewhat lower than the temperature required to produce steam.

The *group* (from Italian *gruppo*) or *brew head* (2) is where the *filter holder* or *portafilter* (3) and metal *filter* (4) clamp, and where the actual brewing takes place. See the cutaway illustration. The pump inside the housing delivers heated water through a perforated plate (*shower head* or *disk*) on the underside of the group, forcing the water through the ground coffee held in the filter and filter holder.

The filter and filter holder can be designed to produce a single or a double serving of espresso. If double, the filter is sufficiently large to contain twice the amount of ground coffee as a single, and the filter holder has two little outlets rather than one.

The *drip tray* (5) catches coffee overflow, and the *steam valve* or *knob* (6) controls the flow of steam through the *steam wand, pipe, or nozzle* (7), which the barista thrusts into the *frothing* or *milk pitcher* (8) to froth and heat milk for cappuccino, caffè latte, and other drinks that combine espresso coffee with hot, frothed milk. The *hot water tap* (9) dispenses hot water for tea and similar hot drinks, and the *cup warmer* (10) stores and gently preheats cups and glasses.

The illustrated machine has a very simple *control panel* (11). A switch above each group turns the brewing water on and off. With such machines the timing of the brewing operation is up to the barista. In machines with more complex controls the barista touches a button to select the length of the shot or serving of espresso (from a single short serving to two long servings). A computer chip does the rest. Controls for fully automatic machines may be even more elaborate, with more options, and may include readouts that provide the barista with information concerning brewing pressure, brew-

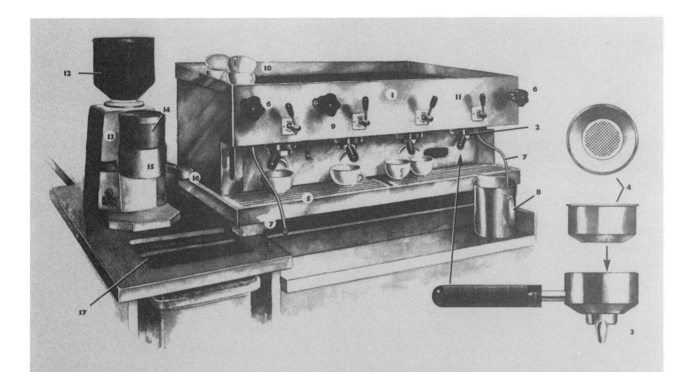

ing temperature, and the like. For illustrated descriptions of more complex machines, see pages 24–30.

On the other hand, manual piston machines (see page 28) provide no control panels or buttons whatsoever. The dose of brewing water is controlled by purely mechanical, nonelectronic means.

The grinder. Note the conical reservoir for roasted whole coffee beans (12), the *grinding unit* proper where the grinding burrs are concealed (13), the *cylinder* where the recently ground coffee is held (14), the *doser* (15), which measures one *dose* or serving's worth of ground coffee at the flick of a lever, and the *tamper, presser,* or *packer* (16), which is used to dis-

tribute and compress the coffee evenly in the filter. Some bar systems may add a second grinder for decaffeinated beans, but if demand for decaffeinated drinks is light, the second grinder may be replaced, as it is here, by a simple container of preground decaffeinated coffee kept close at hand.

The bar. In addition to supporting the machine and grinder, the bar unit also includes a *knock-out* or *dump box* (17), into which the barista disposes spent coffee grounds by inverting the filter holder and knocking it sharply against the edge of the box. The knock-out box may sit atop the counter next to the machine, or it may be built into the structure of the bar, as it is here.

2 CULTURE AND TECHNOLOGY

ESPRESSO HISTORY

From a cultural point of view, the history of espresso extends back several centuries, to the beginnings of Mediterranean coffee-drinking tradition. If we look at espresso history from a more technical point of view, however, the horizon moves closer, either to the nineteenth century and the first use of the trapped pressure of steam to force water through a compressed bed of ground coffee, or to the mid-twentieth century, when Achille Gaggia introduced the first commercial machines to use a spring-loaded piston to force the hot water through the coffee at pressures even greater than could be achieved with trapped steam.

THE CULTURAL CONTEXT

Italians are wont to give the impression that the development of espresso was a purely rational, inevitable process, driven by technical factors alone, aimed at producing the best possible cup of coffee. However, the various North American and European technicians who developed the automatic filter-drip system might make the same argument for the process through which they perfected their brewing method.

Cultures and individuals choose to roast, brew, and drink coffee the way they do for reasons that are largely irrational. There is no intrinsic culinary logic or technical rationale for preferring "Turkish"-style coffee over espresso, for example, or for preferring either espresso or Turkish-style coffee over American-style filter coffee. Each of these coffee-drinking traditions represents a somewhat different cultural definition of "coffee."

A Technical and Sensual Logic

It would seem, however, that once a culture has settled on a collective definition of coffee, a certain technical and sensual logic comes into play. Given the traditional North American definition of coffee, for example, we probably can say that automatic filter-drip coffee is "better" than percolator coffee, because given North American tastes the filter-drip coffee is brighter, clearer, and more aromatic than the percolator coffee, which has been perked to death, as it were. But I doubt whether a coffee drinker from either Yemen or Milan would consider either filter or percolator coffee much better than insipid hot water. Good espresso is neither bright nor clear like North American filter coffee, nor is it somewhat soupy and gritty like Turkish-style brew. Good espresso has its own, particular set of criteria for goodness.

The Idea of Espresso

So we must begin by tracing the taste for the kind of coffee that *became* espresso, for the *idea* of espresso, before we take up the technical developments that brought that taste or idea to perfection.

When coffee first made its appearance in human culture it was almost certainly as a medicinal herb in the natural medicine chest of the peoples of the horn of Africa, in what is now Somalia and Ethiopia. For until sometime in the fifteenth century, when Arab peoples in what is now Yemen learned to take this seed of a humble little berry, roast it, grind it, and combine it with hot water, it doubtless had little appeal to the human senses beyond its effect as stimulant. And even roast, ground, and brewed, coffee is a hard first sell to the taste buds. There is no evidence that I know of indicating that the human organism "likes" the taste of coffee at first encounter, although the aroma may have a natural appeal. Coffee, like many other beverages, appears to be an acquired taste.

Perhaps this is the reason that sugar was added to the cup fairly early in coffee's history. The earliest accounts of coffee brewing in Arabia, Egypt, Syria, and Turkey seem to suggest that, although adding sugar or even milk (most likely goat's milk) to the cup was not unknown, coffee was generally drunk either straight or with the addition of perfume or spice, most often cardamom. The "Turkish" coffee we are familiar with today, in which a finely powdered coffee and varying proportions of sugar are brought to a boil several times in a small pot, then dispensed into tiny cups, apparently took hold in the seventeenth century in Egypt and Turkey. This style of coffee, which eventually came to dominate the coffee cultures of the Middle East, North Africa, and Southeastern Europe, is drunk without separating the grounds from the coffee. The coffee is served very hot, and covered by a head of froth produced by the repeated boiling. By the time the liquid is cool enough to drink, the powdered coffee grounds largely have settled to the bottom of the cup, leaving only a slight, pleasantly bitter suspension of grit in the drink.

Although the differences between a demitasse of Turkish-style coffee and a demitasse of espresso may be rather striking, yet so are the similarities. In both cases, a rather darkly roasted coffee is drunk out of small cups; in both cases the coffee is heavy-bodied and usually taken sweetened; in both cases a good deal of emphasis is placed on the froth that covers the coffee (in the case of espresso the crema, in Turkish-style coffee the *kaymak,* to use the Turkish term).

Cow's Milk and Strained Coffee

It is to Christian Europe's love-hate relationship with the Ottoman Turks that we can attribute both the spread of coffee to Western Europe and the use of the term "Turkish" to describe a style of coffee now drunk over a large part of Eurasia and Africa. Tradition ascribes the habit of adding milk to coffee, which figures so importantly in North America's growing love of espresso cuisine, to the failed siege of Vienna by the Turks in 1683. Franz George Kolschitzky, a Polish hero in the struggle, supposedly opened the first Viennese cafés with coffee left behind by the Turks after the siege was lifted. According to tradition, Kolschitzky first tried to serve his booty Turkish-style, grounds and all, but was forced to innovate by straining the coffee and adding milk to it before luring townspeople into the first of the famous Viennese cafés.

Historians have turned up earlier references to the use of milk in coffee, but in a real, cultural sense, legend is probably correct in attributing the beginning of the practice to Kolschitzky. Other coffee drinkers may have experimented with adding milk to their coffee, but the widespread, popular tradition of drinking strained coffee with cow's milk probably did begin in Vienna in the seventeenth century, and spread from there into Western Europe. Meanwhile the areas of Eastern Europe and the Mediterranean that remained under Ottoman Turk control until later centuries (the Balkans, Hungary, Greece, Egypt, present-day Turkey, Lebanon, etc.) continue until this day to drink coffee in the "Turkish" style. This clear demarcation of coffee-drinking habits, with most people east of Vienna still taking their coffee Turkish-style with grounds, and most regions west of Vienna taking their coffee strained, often with milk, would seem to indicate that the innovation in coffee drinking that took place in Vienna in the seventeenth century was decisive in the history of coffee habits in Western Europe.

A Middle Eastern or "Turkish" coffee set. The object in the middle is the ibrik *(Turkish) or* briki *(Greek), in which finely-powdered coffee, water, and (usually) sugar are brought to a foamy boil. The resulting strong, frothy suspension is poured from the* ibrik *into the little cups.*

Coffee Comes to Italy

Coffee was first imported into Europe on a commercial scale through Venice beginning in the seventeenth century. As a consequence Venice developed Europe's first coffeehouses, one of which, Caffè Florian (1720), is still extant, delighting tourists and lightening them of quantities of *lire*. Although Caffè Florian today serves the classic Italian espresso cuisine, with a latte or two thrown in for the North Americans, the early Venetian caffès almost certainly served coffee in the Turkish style, boiled with sugar and drunk with the grounds settled to the bottom of the cup.

It is doubtless the very powerful Austrian influence in northern Italy in the eighteenth and nineteenth centuries that created a taste for filtered coffee and coffee mixed with milk. Austria controlled Milan, the ultimate center of espresso innovation, from 1714 to 1860, with only a brief interruption of French rule under Napoleon.

Still, it is tempting to see a lingering Turkish influ-

A nineteenth-century depiction of the Caffè Florian in Venice's Piazza San Marco. Founded in 1720, The Caffè Florian was one of Europe's first coffeehouses, and survives today virtually intact.

ence in the modern Italian obsession with crema, the finely textured brown froth that covers the surface of a well-brewed espresso. The culture of Turkish-style coffee puts a similar emphasis on the froth. In both the espresso and Turkish-style coffee cuisines, to serve coffee without a proper covering of froth is a sign of culinary impotence, bad manners, or both.

Nevertheless, it would seem that the Austrian influence is most important in the genesis of espresso, for although Italians continued to enjoy coffee strong, sweetened, and in small cups, the fact that they strained their coffee and often added hot milk to it is of the utmost importance in understanding the development of espresso cuisine.

Liberation of a Coffee Ideal

For it is on this cultural premise, i.e. a taste for coffee that is strong and heavy-bodied, yet filtered, and often combined with hot milk, that the great espresso cuisine of northern Italy developed. It is as though the ideal of espresso was somehow present from the moment northern Italians developed a taste for strong, heavy-bodied, yet filtered coffee. The rest of the technical history of espresso can be seen as a gradual achievement of that goal, a liberating of it, as it were, from the shackles of technical limitation.

In fact, it wouldn't be too much of a stretch to argue that this taste for heavy-bodied yet filtered coffee represents a typically Italian maximization of the two cultural strains—the eastern Mediterranean (Byzantine and Arab) and the Western European—that together have made Italian culture such a continually fascinating and creative blend. The eastern Mediter-

ranean influence is seen in the cultural premise of small cups of heavy-bodied coffee drunk sweetened and covered with froth; the Western European in the practice of filtering the coffee and often combining it with cow's milk, and in the almost obsessive tendency to apply technological innovation to the brewing process.

ENTER TECHNOLOGY

For it is at this point, during the nineteenth century, that the cultural history of espresso also becomes a history of espresso technology. Though tinkering and gadget making has been part of coffee culture almost from its inception, the scale and thoroughness with which espresso cuisine utilizes technology remains unprecedented, and is undoubtedly one of the principal sources of its fascination for the rest of the world.

By the time the industrial revolution spread through Western Europe during the late eighteenth and early nineteenth centuries, coffee drinking was a well-established habit, and it was inevitable that the repetitive, familiar ritual of coffee brewing would provoke the interest of the tinkerers and inventors of the period.

Improving the Filter Pot

The starting point for many of these coffee-making innovations was the familiar drip or filter pot, in which the simple pull of gravity causes hot water to trickle down through a bed of coffee loosely laid over a metal or ceramic filter. There are several drawbacks to the filter-drip method. One is the slowness of the process. If the coffee is ground too finely, the brewing process may even stop altogether, and the impatient coffee lover is forced to knock the pot around or stir the grounds in an effort to speed things up. Not only is the drip method slow, but it is also relatively costly and inefficient, since the rather coarse grind demanded by the method means a less thorough extraction than could be achieved with a finer grind.

For these reasons, some of the more sophisticated efforts to apply the technologies of the early industrial revolution to coffee making expedite the drip process by either pulling the hot water through the problematical bed of ground coffee (via a partial vacuum) or by pushing it through by various expedients, including compressed air, hand-operated plungers, and the pressure of trapped steam.

Pulling and Pushing

By the 1840s the pulling approach was in use in several versions of what is now known as the vacuum brewer, in which a mild vacuum sucks the brewing water down through a bed of ground coffee.

Other coffee-maker tinkerers pursued the opposite approach. Rather than making use of a partial vacuum to pull the hot water through the bed of coffee, their devices applied pressure to the hot water to push it through. Many of these early nineteenth-century designs anticipate solutions applied later in espresso technology. In some devices a hand-operated piston forces water through the bed of coffee. In others, compressed air manually pumped into the hot water chamber provides the brewing pressure.

The method that eventually prevailed in the early espresso technology, however, utilized the trapped pressure of steam. Water brought to a boil inside a sealed chamber created steam; the confined steam then forced the water through the bed of coffee. A glance at the cutaway illustration on page 114 of a simple contemporary Moka-style coffee pot gives a general idea of how these early small steam-pressure devices worked. The first European patents for home devices using the steam-pressure principle were filed between 1818 and 1824. Various ingenious refinements to the steam pressure principle were proposed, forgotten, and proposed all over again throughout the nineteenth century, but all remained either commercially unexploited or applied only to small-scale home brewers. It was not until the early years of the twentieth century that the steam pressure principle was finally successfully applied to a large commercial machine, and the technology and culture of caffè espresso was born.

Precursors of the Espresso Machine

The first large caffè machine to utilize a variation on the steam pressure principle is credited to Édouard Loysel de Santais, who at the Paris Exposition in 1855 demonstrated a machine that used the pressure of trapped steam not to directly force the brewing water through the coffee, but rather to raise the water to a considerable height above the coffee, whence it descended through an elaborate system of tubes to the coffee bed. The weight of the hot water, not the trapped steam, applied the brewing pressure. Santais's complex machine brewed "two thousand cups of coffee in an hour," according to one impressed contemporary observer. It apparently brewed coffee a potful at a time, however, just as many French cafés today still brew their espresso. Despite its impressive technology, Santais's device apparently was too complicated and difficult to operate to have any lasting influence on public coffee making.

Nevertheless, various northern Italians persisted in attempting to improve on machines like Santais's device. Why the northern Italians continued in this effort, when it was largely dropped elsewhere in favor of other coffee-brewing methods, is a matter for speculation. It may be that the Italians, latecomers to the imperialist game and consequently without the coffee-growing colonies possessed by France and England, were forced to compensate for the high cost and relative poor quality of their coffee imports with superior brewing technology. Or it may be that for cultural reasons, perhaps related to the strong eastern Mediterranean influence, Italians simply craved a fuller-bodied cup than North Americans and other Europeans and continued to evolve technology to achieve that end.

The Bezzera Breakthrough

The next important date in the technical development of espresso is 1901, when the Milanese Luigi Bezzera patented a steam-pressure restaurant machine that distributed the coffee through one or more "water and steam groups" *directly into the cup*. In many respects the Bezzera machine established the basic configuration that espresso machines would maintain until the development of today's fully automatic machines. A glance at the illustrations on page 24 reveals the familiar filter holder, the "group" into which the filter holder and filter clamp, the steam valve and wand, etc. The Bezzera design also established the emphasis on freshness and drama characteristic of the espresso system: the coffee is custom brewed by the cup for customers before their eyes. Again, this feature of espresso culture intriguingly suggests another aspect of the Turkish-style coffee culture: in traditional Middle Eastern coffeehouses the coffee is always brewed by the cup, on demand. At any rate, the concept of freshly ground coffee brewed on demand has remained a central element of the espresso system ever since Bezzera's innovation.

The Bezzera patent was acquired by Desiderio Pavoni in 1903, who began manufacturing machines based on the Bezzera design in 1905. Pier Teresio Arduino started producing similar machines soon afterward, and other manufacturers followed. By the 1920s these towering, ornament-topped machines dominated the Italian caffè scene. Initially heat was provided by gas. In fact, it is unlikely that the large steam-pressure machines of the early twentieth century could have prevailed without the availability of gas as a steady, reliable source of heat. It was not until the 1920s and '30s that electricity replaced gas in many machines, encouraging smaller, art moderne versions of the Bezzera design that rapidly heated relatively small quantities of water in more compact boilers.

Espresso-Powered Imagery

The 1920s also was the time in which the imagery of espresso as a symbol of urban speed and energy first emerged. The famous Victoria Arduino poster of

1922 reproduced on page vii sums up these associations: the romantic power of steam drove both locomotive and espresso (espresso machines of the period often literally resemble sleek locomotives set on end), while the sophisticated urbanite, espresso powered as it were, rockets his way on a *tazzina* of coffee through the urban machine without a wasted second. Occasionally the work of the Italian Futurist movement in the midst of its celebration of urban speed and potency betrays a similar association with coffee. The famous 1910 painting by Umberto Boccioni, *Riot in the Galleria,* reproduced on page 18, represents a sort of well-dressed brawl in front of a caffè. It explodes not only with the almost hysterical energy of the city, but with the powerful excitement of coffee (and presumably of the new culture of espresso) as well. Note how light shoots from the caffè like spikes of some frenzied indoor mental sun.

BREAKING THE 1½ ATMOSPHERES CEILING

Throughout the period between the wars, however, there were signs that Italian coffee innovators were not content with the 1½ atmospheres of pressure exerted on the brewing water by trapped steam alone. The pressure could be increased by intensifying the heat and thus the steam pressure, but the intensified heat often cooked or baked the ground coffee during the brewing process. It was also generally known that the boiling point was not the optimum temperature for water used in brewing coffee and that a smoother extraction of the flavor oils could be obtained by a water temperature short of boiling. Both of these concerns argued for a method of applying pressure to the brewing water other than trapped steam.

The most commercially successful of these between-the-wars attempts to increase brewing pressure involved making use of the simple power of water run from the tap. Called "electro-instantaneous" machines, these devices used electric elements to rapidly heat tap water to brewing temperature in miniature boilers, one boiler to each brewing group. Each boiler was separately connected to the tap. When the operator tripped a lever above a group, the pressure of new water introduced from the tap forced the hot water in the boiler out through the ground coffee. Depending on the strength of the local water pressure, such machines could exert considerably more than the 1½ atmospheres generated by steam pressure machines.

These devices maintained the same vertical profile as the steam pressure machines, but were smaller and reflected the art deco and art moderne design trends of the late 1920s and 1930s, with straight lines and dramatic geometries replacing the art nouveau curves of the earlier steam pressure designs.

Other efforts to beat the 1½-atmospheres ceiling involved compressed air. A charming little home machine in the possession of Milanese collector Ambrogio Fumagalli, for example, which dates from between the wars, uses a pump to apply pressure to the brewing water (for an illustration, see page 31). And in 1938, Francesco Illy built the Illetta, a large, sophisticated commercial machine making use of compressed air.

In the same years, however, two coffee tinkerers in Milan were pursuing a direction that would have

In this painting by Umberto Boccioni ("Riot in the Galleria," 1910) dazzling light radiates from a caffè, illuminating a frenzied city scene of the kind favored by the Italian Futurists. It is tempting to see a connection between the new culture of espresso and the nervous urban energy celebrated by the Futurists in paintings like this one.

considerably more impact in espresso history. The details of their story are not entirely clear, but the ultimate outcome is: a new approach to espresso brewing that would completely transform the drink and its technology.

Spring-Powered Espresso

In the years before World War II one Signor Cremonesi patented a device that forced water through the coffee by means of a screwlike piston. When a horizontal lever was turned, it forced the piston

18

downward in a screwing motion, pushing the brewing water, which had been injected between the piston and the filter, down through the coffee. Meanwhile Achille Gaggia, a Milanese caffè owner, was experimenting with a similar device at about the same time. The Gaggia device could be bolted onto other manufacturers' machines, in effect replacing the old steam pressure brewing group with the new screwdown version.

World War II interrupted Cremonesi's and Gaggia's experiments, and during that time Cremonesi died, leaving the rights to his patent to his widow, Rosetta Scorza. It is not clear whether Scorza shared her dead husband's ideas with Gaggia, or whether Gaggia simply proceeded on his own, but at any rate by 1947 Gaggia had taken the original idea of the piston suggested by both inventors, and transformed it into his revolutionary "lever group." Rather than a laborious screw, the piston was now powered by a powerful spring. The operator pulled down a longish lever, which simultaneously compressed the spring and drew hot water into the chamber between the piston and the coffee. As the spring above the piston expanded, it forced the piston down, pushed the hot water through the coffee, and allowed the lever to return majestically to its original erect position. See page 28 for a cross section of a typical spring-piston mechanism.

In 1948 Gaggia brought out the first complete machines to incorporate his new device. They were an almost instant success, and apparently were responsible for the creation of the mystique of the crema in Italian coffee culture. Note the art moderne lines and the logo on the 1948 Gaggia machine pictured on page 25, proclaiming "Crema Caffe/Naturale" ("Natural Coffee Cream"). What constituted "unnatural" coffee cream I have no idea. Perhaps the question could only be asked by a foreigner; the emphasis is clearly on crema as a natural part of the brewing process, an evidence of richness. Historical anecdote suggests that Gaggia's crema slogan was a way of turning a liability into an asset. According to these stories, when people asked what that peculiar scum was floating on their coffee, Gaggia and his associates called it "coffee cream," suggesting that his new method produced coffee that was so rich that, in effect, the coffee produced its very own cream. Whatever the truth of that story, even since Gaggia's time "crema" has become the mark of a properly brewed espresso.

The success of the Gaggia design is understandable. It finally achieved the implicit goal toward which espresso cuisine had been aspiring—the easy richness, smoothness, and full body of classic espresso. It achieved this goal by pushing the brewing water through an even more tightly packed bed of coffee than before, at a much greater pressure than ever before, assuring the rapid, complete extraction of the flavor oils characteristic of the mature espresso method.

A Performance Opportunity

What is less commonly recognized is that the Gaggia-style machines also produced one of coffee's greatest performance opportunities. The muscular pull on the lever and its slow return to an upright position became the signature performance of the barista of the streamlined new espresso bars that replaced the more spacious (and doubtless more gracious) caffès and neighborhood bars of less hurried pre–World War II days. The boilers were smaller in the new machines, and were laid on their sides inside sleek housings, further reinforcing the updated image of speed, power, and modernity projected by the new brewing technology.

One could argue that all developments in espresso technology since Gaggia's breakthrough are mere refinements. Certainly one can make as good an espresso with a piston-style machine as with any later machine, and owing to their simplicity, ease of maintenance, and the control they permit the skilled operator, many piston machines continue to be used. Some of the better caffès in the United States still prefer the piston machines.

Automation and Speed

Nevertheless, since the day of its introduction the effort to improve the Gaggia design has never ceased. In the 1950s the Cimbali company introduced its "Hydromatic" machine, which, like the Gaggia design, used a piston to force the brewing water through the coffee. Unlike the Gaggia design, however, the piston was powered by tap water, which was run into a chamber above and behind the piston. As more and more water entered this chamber, the piston was gradually forced down, in turn pushing the hot brewing water on the underside of the piston through the coffee. This hydraulic brewing operation was controlled "automatically" by a button, hence the name "Hydromatic." The Cimbali Hydromatic is illustrated on page 25. Like the Gaggia design, the hy-

draulic machine is a technological classic that is valued for its sturdy simplicity, and designs almost identical to the original Cimbali machine are still being manufactured and sold.

The Cimbali machines were quickly upstaged by the introduction in 1960 of the famous E61 machine of Ernesto Valente's FAEMA company, the first espresso device to use an electric pump to force the hot water through the coffee. The E61 also incorporated several other recently developed innovations, the most important of which was a method of heating brewing water in small batches by means of a device called a *heat exchanger*. Recall that the Gaggia-style machines heated the water used for both brewing and steam production in a large tank or boiler at the heart of the machine, a feature that presented two disadvantages: the machine was slow to heat to operating temperature, and the water sometimes became saline or stale when held in the tank for long periods. The heat exchanger is a tube that carries fresh water through the tank of already hot, "old" water. As the electric pump pushes fresh water through this tube, it is heated by the surrounding water of the tank, yet is protected by the tube from contamination. Thus it is delivered hot but fresh to the brewing head. Meanwhile, the hot water in the tank is used only for producing steam for milk frothing.

Another of the technical elements that made the Valente design successful was the use of a decalcification process to soften the water before it entered the pump and heating apparatus, thus preventing the mechanism from being fouled by lime deposits. Finally, the Valente design circulated hot water from the tank through concealed cavities in the group or brew head, thus making it unnecessary for the operator to preheat the group by running brewing water through it, as was required by the Gaggia design. The illustration on page 29 indicates the main interior components of the Valente design and its many successors down to the present.

Externally, the Valente FAEMA design replaced the long lever of the Gaggia design with a much smaller lever. The operator, rather than pulling on a long handle, simply activates the pump by tripping the lever, and after a suitable amount of coffee has been pressed into the cup, trips the lever a second time to end the brewing operation.

Like both the Gaggia manual piston and Cimbali hydraulic designs, the FAEMA machine has been an enduring classic. Some of the original machines are still operating, and new machines using virtually the same design continue to be manufactured and sold, though by firms other than FAEMA.

INFORMATION AGE ESPRESSO

The principal developments since the E61 have been in the direction of automation, and as industrial age modulated to information age, the computer and its potential for controlling complex, repeated operations entered the picture. The most prevalent style of machine in Italy and the United States today is usually described as a semi-automatic machine, which simply means it is a refined, push-button version of the Valenti E61. A pump still pushes the instantly heated hot water through the coffee, though the pump and heating operation is usually activated by a button rather than a lever. Many semi-automatic machines incorporate a computer chip and control panel, which regulate the flow of water through the coffee to produce anywhere from a single *corto* or short espresso to a double *lungo* or long espresso. Thus the operator is relieved by the computer of the need to cut off the flow of water through the coffee at the correct moment. For an illustrated description of a typical semi-automatic machine, see page 27.

In the semi-automatic machine, however, the operator still loads the filter with coffee, disposes of the grounds, froths the milk, and assembles the final drink. Beginning in the 1980s, fully automatic machines have appeared, which grind, dose, and tamp the ground coffee, brew it according to the directions punched into the machine by the operator, and dispose of the grounds. With the popularity of decaffeinated coffee, particularly in Switzerland, Germany, and North America, many of the larger automatic machines incorporate two separate grinders, and will produce either decaffeinated or regular espresso, in any increment of quantity, at the touch of a button. Most of these fully automatic machines do not heat and froth the milk and assemble the final drink, however, which is still left to the barista.

Machines That Do It All

Inevitably, machines have been developed that do it all, including frothing the milk and assembling the drinks. Some are modest box-shaped devices that sit atop counters in European offices, and others are muscular coin-operated devices that wait dutifully in airports and waiting rooms. Although these European vending and office machines brew genuine espresso, their milk-frothing function tends to be compromised by various technical expedients.

This was not true with the made-in-USA Acorto 990, the first fully automatic machine to take into account the North American taste for mammoth caffè lattes and other oversized frothed-milk-and-espresso drinks. The Acorto 990 (for an illustrated description, see page 27) and its progeny use fresh, cold milk, and brew the espresso, froth the milk, and assemble the drink in automatic but authentic fashion. Kept in proper running order, the Acorto machines produce espresso cuisine virtually indistinguishable from the production of a good barista working a semi-automatic machine in classic fashion.

However, so far most Italian and North American caffès and bars have stuck with the simpler manual and semi-automatic devices, at most trusting the machine to measure the water and time the brewing but leaving the loading, tamping, frothing, and assembling procedures to the operator. Italian bar operators argue that fully automatic machines cannot be trusted to administer the process with the same precision as a well-trained operator, and many also prefer to avoid the higher maintenance costs attributed to fully automatic machines. Finally, there is the psychological importance of ritual in both Italy and North America. In both cultures, espresso means an experience as well as a beverage, and in Italy, in particular, that experience involves a skillful barista who performs the ritual of espresso with panache, and who can produce customized espresso, with each demitasse perfectly tuned to the individual customer's preferences.

Invisible, Unseen Power

The visual appearance of the fully automatic machines tends to reflect the reticence and gestural understatement of the computer age. Rather than flaunting theatrical ornaments atop an elegant metal tower like the twenties Bezzera/Pavoni machines, or promoting a macho pull on a long phallic handle like the 1950s Gaggia design, the machines of the 1990s present a sleek, understated cabinet and involve minimal theatrics from the operator. The vision of modernity they seem to aspire to is the invisible, unseen power of the computer, rather than the extraverted power of industry suggested by the earlier designs.

Of course we continue to experience the contradictions of the high-tech, high-touch paradox pointed out by Alvin Toffler in his 1970 book, *Future Shock*. At the same historical moment that the espresso machines of the present express the understated, reticent power of the computer, other perfectly ordinary machines come tarted up with copper siding and various irrelevant pipes and gewgaws meant to suggest (to impressionable diners) the *belle époque*, while still others are honest replicas of the famous machines of the recent past, like the FAEMA E61 noted earlier. Thus at the same moment that we reach toward ever greater automation and efficiency, we simultaneously clutch nostalgically at the forms and rituals of the past.

DOMESTIC ESPRESSO

From the introduction of the Bezzera/Pavoni machines at the turn of the century to the present, espresso cuisine has been a largely public phenomenon. Small home devices have usually mimicked the larger machines.

The exception may be the small, steam pressure coffee makers of modest ambition the Italians simply call *caffettiera,* or coffee pots. From the mid-nineteenth century until the present the design of these devices has changed very little. A look at the historical examples on pages 24–25 and the contemporary examples on pages 26–27 together give some idea of the range and persistence of these little devices.

All work on the simple principle of the earliest caffè machines: water is set to boiling by stove, alcohol lamp, or electric element; when steam pressure builds sufficiently inside the water chamber it forces the water through the coffee. There is no steam valve for frothing milk; seldom is there even a means to cut off the flow of coffee. To avoid running too much water through the coffee and ruining it through overextraction, one must resort to expedients—carefully limiting the amount of water put in the reservoir, for example.

Bringing the Bar Home

But parallel to the uneventful history of these eternal little devices has been a steady development of more complex (and more expensive) machines that, as one Italian advertisement puts it, "bring the bar home." And since the machines at the bar have changed over the years, so have the home machines that imitate them.

Examples of these machines are described and illustrated on pages 30–34. Note that most of the developments in the full-sized caffè machines are mirrored here, from the little Gaggia machine with a spring-loaded piston to the Saeco full automatic. The range of aesthetics of the large machines is mirrored as well, from the extraverted steam-engine look of the Europiccola to the no-nonsense reticence of the Saeco Super Automatica Twin.

For those considering purchasing a home machine, I give some advice on pages 30–34. Detailed suggestions on using these devices is provided in Chapter 9.

ESPRESSO BREAK
THE CAFFÈ GIANTS

In Italy the great espresso machines of the past evoke the same rush of admiration and nostalgia that certain old automobiles and jukeboxes do in the United States. The six machines that follow represent key developments and trends in the history of the caffè espresso machine.

La Pavoni espresso machine

1920S AND 1930S

La Pavoni. A machine typical of those manufactured in the 1920s by Pavoni and many other firms. Machines like this one essentially created espresso culture and carried it across Europe and the Americas. Steam pressure is generated in the giant gas-fired boiler (see the cross-section illustration on page 28), which forces hot water through the coffee, held in a filter holder almost identical to those used in machines today. Note, for example, the familiar shape of the group, the filter holder, and the steam wand. Only the lever operating the coffee valve, reminiscent of a steam engine throttle, differs from the various levers and buttons that control coffee output in later machines.

Although these machines forced water through the coffee at a paltry 1½ atmospheres, compared to the 9 or more atmospheres considered ideal today, they introduced several innovations that carried the day for espresso: a richer coffee, brewed under pressure; a fresher coffee, custom brewed by the cup; and milk heated by having steam run through it, eliminating the flat taste acquired by milk heated in the conventional manner. The beauty and drama of these machines, rising above caffè-goers like gleaming towers and surrounded by wisps of steam and elegant ministrations of baristas, undoubtedly further contributed to their success.

1940S AND 1950S

Early Gaggia Spring Piston Machine. Soon after World War II, Achille Gaggia produced the first machine to successfully press hot water through the bed of finely granulated coffee at six to nine times the pressure generated by trapped steam alone. Gaggia's machine used a piston powered by a spring. The spring was compressed by a lever; the barista pulled down the lever, and as the spring-driven piston pressed the water through the coffee the lever returned majestically to its upright position. See the cross-section illustration on page 28.

The slogan on the machine reads "Crema Caffè/ Naturale" ("Natural Coffee Cream"). This slogan refers not to the addition of actual cream to the coffee, but rather to the dense golden froth, or *crema,* "naturally" covering the surface of the espresso, a sign of richness and a symptom of the greater brewing pressure achieved by the new Gaggia design.

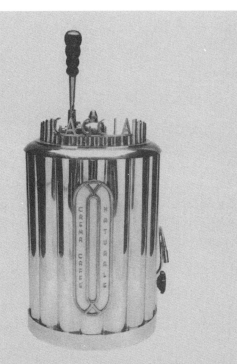

Early Gaggia spring-piston machine

1950S AND EARLY 1960S

Cimbali Hydraulic Machine. In 1956 the Cimbali company introduced the world's first hydraulically powered piston espresso machine. The piston was powered by the simple force of tap water; see the illustration on page 28. The earliest hydraulic machines, like the one on this page, were complex and extraverted in their exterior design, and re-

Cimbali hydraulic machine

quired the operator to closely control the various phases of the brewing cycle. Later versions were almost completely automatic, requiring only the pressing of a switch to initiate the brewing operation.

1960S AND 1970S

The FAEMA E61. The momentous decade of the 1960s was heralded in the espresso world by the introduction of the FAEMA E61, a machine lavish with innovation. The brewing water was heated on demand, rather than held hot in a large tank or boiler; a pump rather than a spring-driven piston supplied the brewing pressure; a decalcification system prevented the pump and heating mechanism from becoming fouled by hard water deposits; and hot water from the boiler, circulating through the group, maintained an even operating temperature in its metal components. Despite the advanced, automated nature of the machine's operation, the group, pictured in the detail illustration, retained some of the complex, romantic look of the brewing apparatus on earlier machines. Brewing was controlled by the little lever to the right of the filter holder.

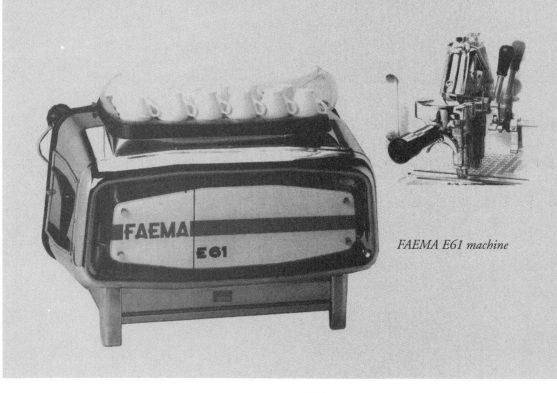

FAEMA E61 machine

1980S AND 1990S

Semi-Automatic and Automatic Machines. The machine on the right is typical of many evolved in the 1980s by numerous manufacturers. The operator still must dose and tamp the coffee, but the brewing process itself is controlled by microchip and button. Note the line of six buttons above each group. In the case of this machine the operator can, from left to right, select a single short serving, a double short serving, a single regular serving, two regular servings, initiate a continuous flow of water through the coffee, or stop the operation entirely. Other machines may present considerably more complex control panels and options.

The U.S.A.-made Acorto 990, illustrated on the right, is a fully automatic machine designed with the North American cuisine in mind. Several European manufacturers also produce fully automatic machines, but most of the European automatics still leave the milk frothing to the barista. The Acorto will produce up to twenty-two different espresso drinks, ranging from short espressos to mammoth caffè lattes, in either regular or decaffeinated versions. Note the twin bean silos, one for regular and one for decaffeinated beans. The machine also incorporates refrigeration for the milk.

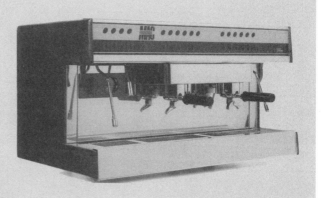

Typical semi-automatic machine: Nuova Simonelli MAC Digit

Acorto 990 machine

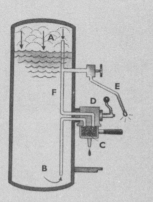

Steam-pressure machine

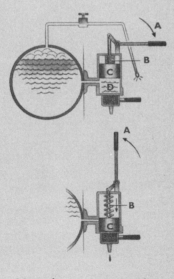

Manual spring-piston machine

NINETY YEARS OF
ESPRESSO TECHNOLOGY

On the left is a cross section of a typical steam pressure machine of the kind popularized by Pavoni and Victoria Arduino in the early part of the twentieth century and described on page 24. The pressure of steam trapped in the gas-fired central boiler (A) presses downward on the hot brewing water (B), forcing it through the compressed bed of coffee (C) when the operator opens a tap (D). The upper part of the boiler is tapped to provide steam for frothed milk drinks through the familiar steam wand (E). Not indicated is the option of directing steam through the spent coffee grounds, so as to dry them into tidy cake that pops out of the filter without clumsy digging or rinsing. This step was not incorporated in later machine designs because the stronger brewing pressure generated by more advanced machines tended to compress and dry the spent grounds automatically.

The famous Gaggia manual spring-piston machine (page 25) was introduced soon after World War II. The drawing on the left shows a cross section of a brewing group in such a machine. When the operator depresses the lever (A), a spring (B) is compressed above the piston (C), drawing hot water into the cylinder (D) below the piston. The spring then forces the piston back down, pressing the hot water through the bed of ground coffee. The hot water is drawn from a tank similar to the boiler in the Pavoni steam pressure machine, although in most manual piston machines the boiler is laid on its side inside a streamlined housing. As with the Pavoni design, the boiler also provides steam for milk frothing.

The first hydraulic espresso machine was introduced by the Cimbali company in 1956. Like the Gaggia-style spring-piston machines, the hydraulic machines use a piston to force the hot water through the coffee bed. However, in the Cimbali and later hydraulic designs the piston is powered by tap water, and the long lever replaced by a switch. See the illustration on the right, a cross-section detail of a typical hydraulic brewing group. The diagram appears complex at first glance, but represents a simple operating principle: tap water introduced alternately above and below the large piston forces it up and down. The large piston drags the smaller piston below with it, and the smaller piston forces the hot water through the coffee.

When the operator activates the switch beginning the brew cycle, the valve at (E) allows *tap* water (not hot water from the tank) to enter the *larger* cylinder at (A), forcing the larger piston (B) upward. The larger piston lifts the smaller piston (C), allowing hot water from the tank to enter the small cylinder at (D). When the appropriate volume of brewing water has flowed into the small cylinder, a mechanical trigger is tripped, directing the valve at (E) to route tap water into the larger cylinder *above* the piston at (F). This new influx of water forces the large piston down, pushing the tap water below the piston out, and forcing the hot water in the smaller cylinder down through the coffee. The Cimbali hydraulic design, like the Gaggia spring-loaded manual, has proven to be a classic, and machines utilizing the principle continue to be manufactured.

However, the future, or at least a large part of it, belonged to the electric pump design introduced in 1960 by the FAEMA

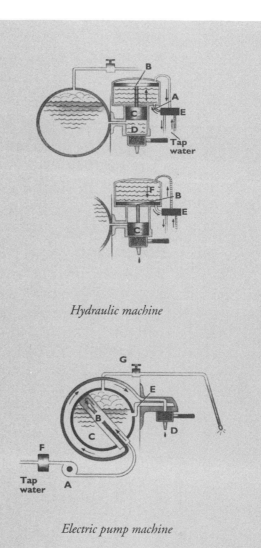

Hydraulic machine

Electric pump machine

company. The basic configuration of the FAEMA E61 is still used in the majority of caffè espresso machines manufactured in the world today. A cross section typical of such machines is represented on the preceding page. Here an electric rotary pump (A) rather than piston provides the brewing pressure. The pump forces cold water into a heat exchanger (B), a largish tube that is surrounded by the hot water of the familiar boiler (C). The cold water inside the exchanger is heated by the surrounding hot water, but is untouched by it, and is forced by continued pressure from the pump into the brewing group (D) and through the coffee. Steam for frothing continues to be supplied by the boiler. A line from the boiler (E) also maintains uniform heat in the brewing group with a convection current of hot water, and a water softening unit (F) keeps the pump and lines from becoming fouled with mineral deposits. Steam for milk frothing is supplied in the usual way by tapping the top of the boiler (G).

In pump machines manufactured today electronic instrumentation often controls the volume and temperature of the brewing water. Some machines may substitute a second boiler in place of the heat exchanger so as to maintain greater control over brewing temperature. Fully automatic machines grind, load, and tamp the coffee for brewing. And the Acorto 990 described on page 27 even froths the milk and combines it with the coffee before dispensing the finished drink. Nevertheless, all of these sophisticated machines are built around the fundamental electric pump technology introduced in 1960 by the FAEMA E61.

E S P R E S S O B R E A K
A C E N T U R Y O F H O M E E S P R E S S O B R E W E R S

AT HOME IN ITALY: EARLY STEAM PRESSURE BREWERS
Italian Steam Pressure Brewer (illustrated page 31). A design typical of many small tabletop brewing devices manufactured in northern Italy throughout the late nineteenth and early twentieth centuries. An alcohol lamp heated water in a sealed reservoir at the lower part of the device. The pressure of steam trapped in the reservoir gradually forced the water up a tube and through a bed of coffee. The brewed coffee exited from the top of the pot via the curved tube into a cup placed next to the machine.

Steam Pressure Brewer with Separate Coffee Chamber (illustrated page 31). In the later nineteenth century steam pressure designs appeared that separated the filter containing the coffee from the water-steam reservoir to avoid baking the ground coffee. Most of these devices presented a profile similar to this early twentieth-century design from the collection of Ambrogio Fumagalli. The water-steam reservoir is at the right. The trapped steam pressure in the reservoir forced the water up and along the horizontal tube at the top of the device, then down through the coffee held in the filter chamber on the left.

This example incorporates an additional useful feature: a

valve controlling the flow of hot water from the reservoir to the filter holding the coffee, which permitted the user to stop the brewing process at will. In the illustration, the control valve appears as a small lever at the top of the reservoir.

CRANKING UP THE BREWING PRESSURE AT HOME

Compressed Air Pressure Brewer (illustrated page 32). In this unusual device from the 1920s, the pressure of compressed air forced the brewing water through the ground coffee. Hot water was placed in the elevated central reservoir. The water was then forced through the ground coffee by means of air pumped into the top of the reservoir by the small hand pump protruding from the base on the left. A concealed tube conducted the air to the top of the reservoir. The ground coffee was held near the bottom of the reservoir in a metal filter.

Gaggia Spring-Loaded Piston Brewer (illustrated page 32). Doubtless an effort by Gaggia to extend the popularity of its revolutionary new lever-operated commercial machines (see page 25) to the home market, this machine from the 1950s used a spring-loaded piston to force hot water through the tightly packed coffee, producing a near caffè-quality espresso. When the handles on either side of the device were clamped down, a spring was compressed inside the top of the central tower. The spring then forced a piston down through a reservoir filled with electrically heated water, pressing the water through the coffee, which was held in a commercial-style filter and filter holder at the bottom of the device. (Also from the collection of Ambrogio Fumagalli.)

Italian steam-pressure brewer

Steam-pressure brewer with separate coffee chamber

Pavoni Europiccola. A charming device still being manufactured, the Europiccola combines the *belle époque* look of the early Pavoni bar machines with a manually operated lever reminiscent of the Gaggia machines of the 1950s. The lever does not compress a spring, however, as in the Gaggia-style

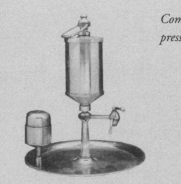

Compressed air pressure brewer

Gaggia spring-loaded piston brewer

Pavoni Europiccola brewer

machines, but directly acts on the piston. In other words, the operator simply leans on the lever and presses the water through the coffee.

STEAM PRESSURE BREWERS: 1950S TO THE PRESENT

"Atomic" Steam Pressure Brewer (illustrated page 33). Both the name "Atomic" and the shape—simultaneously reminiscent of a mushroom cloud and an overstuffed sofa—mark this device as a product of the 1950s, although similar designs had been produced earlier in the century by the same manufacturer. A stovetop machine, the Atomic used the pressure of trapped steam to force the hot water through a detachable, commercial-style filter and filter holder. The addition of a steam valve and wand for making drinks with frothed milk is unusual; most small European home espresso brewers did not, and still do not, incorporate this feature, since most Italians prefer their espresso without milk.

The addition of the steam valve made this device a strong seller in the United States and Australia in the 1960s, when espresso drinks with milk were first becoming popular in both countries. My first two home espresso brewers were Atomics, and I still feel a pang of nostalgia when I see one. The manufacturer of the Atomic is now out of business. It was a rather cranky design that required an attentive operator and some crafty improvisation to produce decent espresso. The small electric countertop devices popular today are easier to use.

The illustrated example comes from the collection of the

Thomas Cara family, San Francisco. Thomas Cara, a pioneering West Coast importer and distributor of espresso apparatus, customized many of the Atomic brewers he sold by adding the little steam pressure gauge seen here protruding from the top of the machine.

Braun Espresso Master. Little electric countertop machines like this one from Braun, and similar models from Krups and other manufacturers, are changing the way North Americans make their coffee. Used carefully, these relatively inexpensive devices can make decent espresso drinks with frothed milk and weak but passable straight espresso. They use the pressure of trapped steam to force the water through the coffee, just as does the Atomic machine above and the earlier devices illustrated on page 32, but they employ an electric element to heat the water and incorporate a steam wand for frothing milk and a valve for stopping the flow of coffee at the optimum moment to avoid overextraction. Machines like this one are a good place to start for caffè latte lovers who want to do it at home. Like many of these small machines, the Braun Espresso Master incorporates a gadget on the end of the steam wand designed to help the neophyte successfully froth milk.

HOME PUMP MACHINES OF THE 1980S AND 1990S

Baby Gaggia (illustrated page 34). This Gaggia machine from about 1980 typifies the first wave of small home pump machines to reach the North American market. It was enor-

"Atomic" steam-pressure brewer

Braun Espresso Master

Baby Gaggia home espresso machine

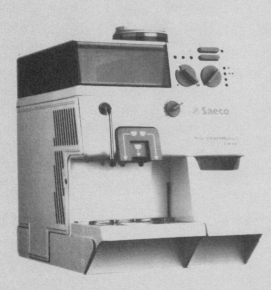

Saeco Super Automatica Twin

mously successful, particularly in Italy, where few urban newlyweds found themselves without a Baby Gaggia after the wedding presents had been opened. Sturdy and authoritative with its clean lines and cast-metal case, it attempted to bring into the home the capabilities of the semi-automatic pump machines that had come to dominate the caffè scene in the 1970s and '80s.

Most of today's home pump machines tend to be smaller, lighter in weight, and cheaper, but they work in the same way. Water is held in a removable, refillable reservoir, and flows as needed into a small boiler, where it is heated to brewing temperature and forced by means of a vibrating electric pump through the ground coffee held in a caffè-style filter and filter holder. Steam for milk frothing is produced by the same boiler, but only after a transitional procedure in which the temperature in the boiler is raised sufficiently to produce a sturdy flow of steam. See page 116 for a cross section of a typical home pump machine.

Saeco Super Automatica Twin. The Saeco Super Automatica Twin and its somewhat smaller relative, the Rio Automatica, were the first fully automatic home machines to be marketed in the United States. Both operated much like the Baby Gaggia described above, but they also ground the coffee, loaded it, tamped it, and after the brewing operation disposed of the grounds, all at the touch of various buttons. Saeco automatic home machines that look and work about the same as the Super Automatica continue to be sold in the United States under different model names.

3 *RISTRETTO* TO *MONDO*

ESPRESSO DRINKS

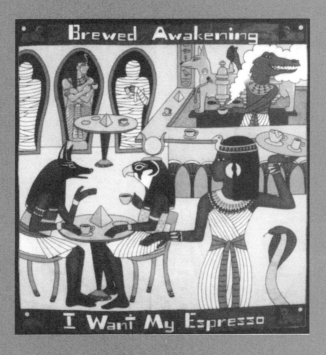

Espresso is more than simply a way to make coffee—it is an entire coffee cuisine. And as espresso technology has been adopted by cultures outside Italy, that one cuisine has become many cuisines. The components that go into these cuisines are simple, however: coffee, always brewed by the espresso method; milk (or milk substitutes); and finally various flavorings added to the drink, at one time only chocolate, but in the United States an increasing (and often bewildering) variety of syrups and garnishes.

THE THREE CUISINES

I've chosen to describe three of these cuisines: the classic northern Italian, the Italian-American, and a new, thoroughly American cuisine that has erupted in many-flavored splendor out of Seattle over the past decade and a half, and has come to dominate the American experience of espresso. This last tradition could be called postmodern espresso, Seattle-style espresso, cart espresso (after the ubiquitous Seattle espresso cart), mall espresso, or even latte espresso, after its featured drink. I should add that Seattle, which recently has become one of the meccas of North American coffee culture, produces some of the purest and most elegantly presented espresso cuisine in the world. However, it also has spawned an innovating new cuisine that has about the same relationship to classic espresso as the pop singer Madonna has to her namesake. Starbucks has adopted a restrained version of the Seattle cuisine, and is busy initiating the rest of the world into its milky ways.

I've described the drinks involved in the three cuisines later in this chapter. Here, however, is an overview.

The Italian Cuisine

Here the emphasis is, above all, on the coffee. There are two principal drinks: a tiny cup of straight espresso, either small, smaller, or smallest, and an austere and splendid cappuccino, the classic drink in which a single serving of fresh, exquisitely brewed espresso is topped with just enough hot milk and milk froth to allow the perfume of the coffee to penetrate every molecule of the cup. The Italian equivalent of the ubiquitous American caffè latte is the *latte macchiato,* milk "stained" or marked with espresso, much smaller than the American latte, but similar in concept: hot milk and a little froth combined with espresso in a tall glass. Not many of these drinks are served in the average Italian bar, however, and the glass tends to hold 6 to 10 ounces, not the mammoth 16 ounces of the usual American latte glass. Caffè latte does not appear on the menus of Italian espresso bars except in places that attract American tourists. In Italian homes a drink called caffè latte may be made with ordinary coffee from the caffettiera and milk heated on the stove, but the perfection of the Italian bar espresso would never be ruined with the amount of hot milk the American espresso culture dumps into it. It goes without saying that the mammoth concoctions of the Seattle cuisine, double and triple servings of espresso sloshed in enough milk to satisfy a kindergarten class, are seldom if ever seen in Italian bars and caffès.

In addition to espresso drinks, Italian bars and caffès, particularly those associated with bakeries, offer an amazing hot chocolate. This is a chocolate beyond rich; it is a chocolate drinker's apocalypse. There is a saying in Italy to the effect that hot chocolate is only acceptable if the spoon stands up in it. This drink, if one can call it that, is often served topped with whipped cream, which makes it resemble a hot fudge sundae without the ice cream. However, a drink combining hot chocolate and espresso similar to the American caffè mocha does not appear to be offered in Italian bars and caffès. It apparently once was; I ran across several references to such beverages in the Italian literature on chocolate. A writer mentions with fond nostalgia the *barbagliata* once offered in Milanese caffès, for example, and the Turinese *bicierin*, apparently both combinations of chocolate and coffee. I suspect that such drinks, together with the caffè latte, went out of style as the small, sleek espresso bar replaced the larger, more leisurely caffè after World War II, and as the espresso machine and its peculiarly Italian "less is more" aesthetic was perfected.

The Italian-American Cuisine

The Italian-American cuisine is my name for that traditional menu of espresso drinks that was developed in Italian-American communities during the 1920s and '40s, moved from there into bohemian and university communities via the American coffeehouses and its various offshoots during the 1950s, and by the 1960s had been taken up by the specialty coffee culture, that world of small boutique coffee roasters and burlap-decorated stores that has now grown to become a major part of the American coffee industry.

The Italian-American cuisine at first glance resembles the contemporary Italian. There are a few more choices on the menu: in particular the caffè latte and the caffè mocha, or chocolate-espresso combination. Otherwise the list is similar: espresso, *ristretto,* or short espresso, cappuccino, etc. The drinks are usually larger, and the servings of straight espresso most definitely larger. But what sets the two cuisines apart more than anything else is the style of the coffee. In the United States, with high-quality Arabica coffees cheap and widely available, espresso blends tend to be sharp and pungent. In Italy, where the cost of coffee is higher and coffee drinkers prefer to take their espresso without milk, the emphasis is on smoother, lighter-flavored blends based on lower-grown Brazil coffees and bland but full-bodied robusta beans. Finally, American espresso blends, particularly on the West Coast, tend to be roasted darker than the northern Italian norm, further accentuating the more rugged flavor profile of American espressos.

Perhaps the most striking difference between the two cuisines is the rituals that surround them in public places, rituals that affect, and in turn are affected by, technical and flavor factors. In Italy, every facet of the brewing and serving ritual is focused on what might be called the *perfect swallow:* The coffee is ground fresh, just before brewing; a small amount is brewed in about 20 seconds into a tiny, preheated cup; and then, before this little liquid jewel can cool or the delicate aromatics liberated by the brewing can evaporate, it is drunk in a few rapid swallows.

Even the time it takes for a waiter or waitress to pick up an espresso and deliver it to a table probably halves the flavor potential in the cup. The premium the espresso system places on immediate consumption of the drink doubtless contributed to the trend in Italy toward the small, streamlined espresso bar that replaced the larger caffè or neighborhood bar of pre–World War II days, with its more unhurried rituals. Certainly other factors predominated in this development, including the rising cost of real estate and the faster pace of life after the war. Nevertheless, the new Gaggia brewing system introduced in the 1950s encouraged drinking the coffee immediately and quickly, to take full advantage of the extraordinary flavor perfumes liberated by the new machines.

By comparison, the Italian-American cuisine was developed and continues to thrive in a much more leisurely context. The American customers' favorite drinks tend to be those that combine hot, frothed milk with the espresso coffee, so a serving lag between brewing and drinking is less important. For years these same customers were primarily artists, bohemians, university students, professionals with irregular work schedules, etc., all of whom not only paid for an espresso beverage, but in effect rented a table as well, where they were free to read a newspaper, write a poem, work on a term paper, or chat with a client in a comfortable and (depending on the social context) defiantly funky or nostalgically European atmosphere.

Think as well about the fundamental tradition of American coffee drinking: the expectation of the bottomless cup, the tradition of sipping relatively weak, often stale coffee for hours on end while occupied with work and talk. Contrast that ritual with the one developed in the Italian espresso bar, where customers stop everything for a few moments to take three or four explosively flavorful swallows of coffee, then immediately return to work or play, riding the resonance of flavor and stimulation. The moment an Italian takes his or her espresso is a brief, but utterly private moment, however public in context; you can tell by the eyes that it is a moment of silent communion between soul and coffee. Then the cup is returned to saucer or saucer to counter, decisively, with a single clack, like an exclamation point, signaling the return of the soul (vigorously) to whatever worldly matters face it.

Once an Italian picks up an espresso cup, it stays in hand until the little golden pool of elixir is completely consumed. By contrast, we Americans like to wrap ourselves around our coffee; nurse it; sip it; psychologically bathe in it. Thus it is no wonder that the Americanized Italian cuisine is longer and taller and milkier.

The Postmodern Cuisine

The same expansive tendency is even more spectacularly in evidence in the postmodern Seattle-style cuisine, where customers can order a triple serving of espresso in a *mondo,* or milkshake-sized container of hot frothed milk, perhaps further enriched by a shot of mint syrup and several kinds of garnishes. The rituals of the new postmodern espresso reveal additional differences from the traditional Italian and Italian-American cuisines. If the small standup bar is the quintessential Italian setting for espresso cuisine, and the café, with tables, chairs, newspapers, and light foods, is the typical setting for the Italian-American cuisine, then the espresso cart is the characteristic setting for the Seattle-style cuisine.

With the espresso cart the cup, saucer, and glass have been dispensed with, and replaced by a disposable cup, either plastic foam or paper. The customers range from those types who also inhabit the traditional café—the newspaper readers, two-hour talkers, and poetry writers—to professionals and clerks who are taking their coffee break outside and on the run, rather than inside, in the office lounge or at their desk. Everything tends to be improvised and casual, and the social space around the cart is continually created and recreated by those who stand, sit, stroll, or dash back to work balancing 16 ounces of espresso drink atop a pile of manila file folders. The carts may vaguely resemble Italian espresso bars, but the customers usually walk away with their tall, milky drinks, rather than down them immediately with an elbow on the bar.

As for the post-modern cuisine itself, it represents the expansive, defiantly nontraditional, and individualistically improvising spirit of western America at its iconoclastic best. It is a cuisine of extremes, from tall, milky, weak drinks in which the espresso can barely be detected amid the pop seductions of pomegranate or pineapple-coconut syrup, to austerely macho "triples" of straight espresso; from the skim milk latte made with decaffeinated coffee to a double *breve,* which delivers two servings of caffeine plus all of the butterfat floating around in 12 ounces of half and half.

It is clear that with the development of the Seattle-style cuisine, with its vigorous pop interpretations of traditional drinks coupled with a sophisticated grasp of espresso technique, espresso in America has finally departed the elitist preserve of imitation Europeans, fancy food freaks, university students, artists, and urban professionals, and is on its way into the mainstream American life.

THE CAFFÈ CUISINES IN DETAIL

What follows is a description of the various beverages that make up the espresso cuisines of the United States and northern Italy. A few words on the Cuban and other Latin American cuisines appears on pages 47–48, but I have not included purely Latin American espresso drinks here for reasons of space and coherence.

For a detailed discussion of assembling the espresso cuisine in the home, see Chapter 9 and related Espresso Breaks. For advice on choosing espresso coffees, see Chapter 6.

The Classic Drinks

Espresso. One-third (Italy) to two-thirds (United States) of a demitasse of espresso coffee, or 1 to 2 ounces, black, usually drunk with sugar.

Espresso Romano (United States; Italian-American). Espresso served with a twist of lemon on the side.

Espresso Ristretto. (United States), **Corto** (Italy), **Short** (Pacific Northwest). The restricted or short espresso carries the "small is beautiful" espresso philosophy to its ultimate: The flow of espresso is cut short at about ¾ ounce or less than a third of a demitasse (Italy) to 1¼ ounces or one-half of a demitasse (United States), producing an even denser, more perfumy cup of espresso than the norm.

Espresso Lungo (Italy, United States), **Long** (Pacific Northwest). A "long" espresso, filling about two-thirds or more of a demitasse. A term not much used in the United States, since most American espresso servings are already long by Italian standards.

Espresso con Panna (Italy, United States). A single or double serving of espresso topped with whipped cream in a 6-ounce cup, usually topped by a dash of unsweetened chocolate powder.

Double (United States), **Doppio** (Italy). Double serving, or about 2½ ounces (Italy) to 3 to 5 ounces (United States) of straight espresso, made with twice the amount of ground coffee as a single serving.

Cappuccino. One serving (about 1¼ ounces in Italy, up to 2 ounces in the United States) of espresso, topped by hot milk and froth. In the classic Italian-American cuisine, a good cappuccino consists of about one-third espresso, one-third milk, and about one-third rather stiff foam, in a heavy 6-ounce cup. In Italy, the milk is not frothed as thoroughly as in the United States, and is presented as a heavier, soupy foam that picks up and combines with the espresso, rather than floating on top of it, as is often the case with the lighter, drier froth typical of American production. The hot, frothed milk is always added *to* the coffee in the cappuccino. Like most espresso drinks, the cappuccino is usually drunk with sugar.

This popular drink is often customized, both in the United States and in Italy. It is not unusual to hear an Italian order a cappuccino *senza spuma,* "without froth," and Americans versed in the ways of Seattle-style espresso have the option of ordering their cappuccino *wet,* with heavy froth, or *dry,* with mostly hard, buoyant froth and little milk.

In less sophisticated American caffès and restaurants a cappuccino can be almost anything, from what in Italy would be a weak latte macchiato to astounding concoctions in which the coffee is so thin and overextracted that it tastes like a solution of burned rubber, the milk is nearly boiled, and the froth is as stiff as overcooked meringue.

Caffè Latte (United States). In the United States, one or two shots of espresso and about three times as much hot milk, in a big bowl or wide-mouthed glass, topped with a short head of froth. Caffè latte has a greater proportion of milk to coffee than a cappuccino does, and tastes weaker and milkier. Strictly speaking, the milk and coffee should be poured simultaneously, from either side of the bowl or glass.

Such combinations of hot milk and coffee have long been the favored breakfast drink of southern Europeans, although the term caffè latte itself appears to be little used in Italy, where those who want a breakfast coffee with more milk than froth usually order a latte macchiato, or perhaps a cappuccino without

The five principal drinks of the classic Italian-American espresso cuisine. Clockwise, from the bottom: espresso, in 3-ounce cup properly half-filled with rich, crema-topped coffee; caffè mocha, in 6-ounce mug, as it was originally served in Italian-American caffès of the 1950s and '60s; caffè latte in 16-ounce glass; latte macchiato in 10-ounce glass; and the classic cappuccino in 6-ounce cup.

foam. In fact, a sure way to reveal that you are an American in Italy is to order a cappuccino after lunch, or a caffè latte at any time. In the United States, caffès often distinguish between caffè latte (made with espresso) and *café au lait,* which substitutes ordinary American filter coffee for the espresso.

Espresso Macchiato (Italy, United States). A serving of espresso "stained" with a small quantity of hot, frothed milk. Served in the usual espresso demitasse.

Latte Macchiato (Italy, United States). A glass filled with hot frothed milk, into which a serving of espresso has been slowly dribbled. The coffee colors, or stains, the milk. In both Italy and the United States, this drink is presented with a relatively short head of froth. Note that in the cappuccino, the milk and froth are added to the coffee, in the caffè latte they are poured simultaneously into a large bowl or glass, mixing them, while in the latte macchiato, the espresso is poured into the milk and froth, creating a layered effect as viewed through the serving glass.

Caffè Mocha (United States), **Moccaccino** (Starbucks). Not to be confused with Mocha Java, a traditional medium-roasted blend of Mocha and Java coffees. In the classic Italian-American espresso cuisine a caffè mocha is one serving (ideally 1¼ ounces) of espresso, mixed with about 2 ounces of very strong hot chocolate, topped with hot frothed milk. The milk is added last, and the whole thing is usually served in an 8-ounce mug. With a classic mocha the hot chocolate is made very strong, so it can hold its own against the espresso and milk. With increasing frequency American caffès simply add chocolate fountain syrup to a caffè latte and call it a mocha. So be it. The mocha does not appear on Italian espresso menus, although the drink is probably based on various coffee-chocolate drinks once popular in northern Italy.

Garnishes and Whipped Cream. In both the Italian and classic Italian-American cuisines, the froth of the cappuccino is garnished with a dash of unsweetened cocoa, which adds a subtle chocolate perfume to the drink. Don't be intimidated by provincial American purists who claim chocolate on a cappuccino is unsophisticated. They haven't been to Italy. Some American establishments use cinnamon as well, which is definitely not done in Italy. I don't care for cinnamon on a cappuccino; I find the flavor too sharp and out of harmony with the dark tones of the coffee. Straight espresso is delicious with whipped cream (*con panna* in Italy), but topping a good, frothy cappuccino with whipped cream is as pointless as putting catsup on red-sauced spaghetti.

Postmodern Espresso, or America Embraces the Machine

Americans have begun to subject the classic espresso cuisine to their own brand of cultural innovation. In general, it would seem that we are frustrated by the brevity and simplicity of the classic Italian and Italian-American cuisines and want bigger drinks with more in them. Perhaps an ounce and a half of coffee in a tiny cup does lack comfort in the middle of the Great Plains or atop the World Trade towers. Still, I think it would be better if Americans understood and experienced the intensity and understated perfection of the classic espresso cuisines before immediately expanding them, watering them down, or adding flavored syrups and ice to them. At any rate, here are some of the more honorable results of American espresso cuisine innovation.

The majority of these creations appear to have originated in Seattle, where a passion for Italian coffee and a shortage of actual Italians seem to have fueled a veritable orgy of home-grown espresso creativity.

Americano. A single serving of espresso with hot water added to fill a 6-ounce cup. Note that simply running 6 ounces of hot water through a single dose of ground coffee will *not* produce an Americano, but will produce 6 ounces of thin, bitter, overextracted espresso. The Americano allows a regular 1¼-ounce serving of espresso to preserve its integrity and perfume, while stretching it to 5 or 6 ounces by adding the hot water.

Depth Charge. A cup of drip coffee with a single shot of espresso dropped into it. Definitely a stealth drink.

Double Cappuccino (or *double cap,* as in baseball cap). If this innovation is made correctly, you should get no more than 3 ounces of uncompromised espresso, brewed with double the usual amount of ground coffee, topped with 3 to 5 ounces of hot milk and froth, with emphasis on the froth. Usually served in an 8- to 10-ounce cup or mug. If the ground coffee is not doubled, and the operator simply forces twice as much water through one serving's worth of ground coffee, you're getting a bitter, watery perversion, rather than a taller, stronger version of a good drink.

Triple Cappuccino. Simply three cappuccinos, usually served in a 12-ounce mug or 16-ounce glass, made with three doses of ground coffee. On behalf of the medical establishment, I should point out that this drink is probably not good for one's health.

Double Caffè Latte. The amount of ground coffee is doubled and the amount of coffee brewed is doubled. Usually, the amount of hot milk and froth remains about the same as in a single caffè latte, or enough to fill a 16-ounce glass. Consequently, a double caffè latte is usually a stronger tasting drink than a single, but represents the same volume of liquid. As with the single caffè latte, the head of froth should be modest, and the drink still relatively milky.

Triple Caffè Latte. See above. Simply a very strong caffè latte, made with three servings of espresso brewed with a triple dose of ground coffee, together with enough hot milk and froth to fill a 16-ounce glass.

Mocha Latte. A taller, milkier version of the classic mocha (see above). If I were to suggest proportions for this invention, they would be one part properly strong espresso, one part properly strong chocolate, and three parts milk and froth. These proportions produce a drink that is milkier, taller, and more muted than the classic mocha, but still rich enough to satisfy.

White Chocolate Mocha, Mocha Bianca. A caffè mocha made with white chocolate. Traditionally, sweet white baking chocolate is melted in a double boiler, combined with milk, and used in place of the normal chocolate concentrate in the caffè mocha. Some companies are now producing white chocolate fountain syrups especially formulated for this drink.

Apparently Berkeley, not Seattle, gave birth to this sweet, delicate version of the classic drink.

Café au Lait. In some American cafés, a drink made with about half American-roast, filter coffee, and about half hot milk and froth, usually served in a 12- or 16-ounce glass or bowl. The proportion of coffee to milk has to be larger than with the espresso-based caffè latte, because American filter coffee is so delicate in flavor and light in body compared to espresso.

Latte by the Ounce. Thanks to Starbucks and imitators, this gas station approach to espresso service is becoming the standard in the United States. The customer specifies the number of shots of espresso (from single through quad, or four), the volume of milk or milk substitute (short, 8 ounces; tall, 14 ounces; grande, 16 ounces; venti or mondo, 20 or 24 ounces), and the kind of milk (no-fat, low-fat, regular, extra-rich, soy, etc.). These drinks are typically delivered with all the elegance of a service station pumping gas, usually into paper or plastic foam cups.

Breve. Seattle-originated term for a caffè latte made with frothed half and half.

Flavored Caffè Latte. The new American espresso cuisine's most ubiquitous and purist-offending invention is the flavored latte, in which a caffè latte is transformed into a chocolate-mint latte, grenadine latte, cherry latte, or any number of other lattes, each through the addition of a dollop of the relevant Italian fountain syrup. The flavored caffè latte, made correctly (about ½ to 1 ounce of syrup to every serving of espresso and approximately 8 ounces of hot milk), should strike a judicious balance between the milk-muted bite of the espresso and the seduction of the syrup.

Eggnog Latte. Seattleites and their fellow decadent celebrants toast the holiday season with this combination of espresso and hot frothed eggnog.

Flavored Frothed Milk, Steamer, Moo. Essentially, a flavored caffè latte without the espresso. One-half to 1 ounce of Italian-style syrup flavoring in about 8 ounces of hot frothed milk, served with a modest head of froth in a caffè latte glass.

The Latte Meets the Soda Fountain, or Syrup-Oriented Variations. These are further elaborations of the flavored caffè latte, and may involve ice cream, whipped cream (often flavored with Italian-style syrups), and topped with everything from maraschino cherries to nuts and M&Ms. All in addition to the flavored frothed milk (and yes, the espresso is in there somewhere). Some of us would prefer espresso baristas to distinguish themselves with flawless espresso and perfect cappuccino, but we're probably the same killjoys who order vanilla ice cream when we could get Cherry Garcia. For suggestions on exploring the soda fountain espresso cuisine at home, see page 133.

The Latte Meets the Health Bar, or Health-Oriented Variations. All over the United States, and particularly in Seattle, any number of custom variations are carried out on the classic drinks, particularly caffè latte, all designed to mute the presumed health hazards presented by the classic cuisine. Drinks are made with skim milk, with 1 percent milk, with 2 percent milk, and with soy milk. They are also made with decaffeinated coffee, and with various coffee substitutes. During the mid-1990s Seattle espresso carts devised an amusing set of jargon for health-oriented espresso drinks, including *Tall Skinny,* a tall caffè latte made with nonfat or 1 percent milk; *Tall Two,* a tall caffè latte made with 2 percent milk; *No Fun,* a caffè latte made with decaffeinated espresso; and *Double No Fun,* the same, with a double serving of decaffeinated espresso.

Iced Espresso. This is usually a double espresso, poured over plenty of crushed, not cubed, ice, in a smallish fancy glass. Some caffès top the iced coffee with whipped cream. Caffès that brew and refrigerate a pitcher of espresso in advance when they feel a hot morning on the way fail to deliver the brewed-fresh perfume of true espresso, but the practice still makes a fine drink, and one that doesn't need to be iced and diluted as much as the version made with fresh espresso.

Iced Cappuccino. Best made with a single or double serving of freshly brewed espresso poured over crushed ice, topped with an ounce or two of cold milk, then some froth (not hot milk) from the machine to top it off. This drink should always be served in a glass. The triple contrast of coffee, milk, and froth, all bubbling around the ice, makes a pleasant sight on a hot day.

Espresso Granita. Traditional Italian-American granitas are made by freezing strong, unsweetened, or lightly sweetened espresso until it is slushy, removing it from the freezer, mixing it, putting it back in the freezer again, and repeating this process until a wonderfully grainy consistency is achieved. This strong, dark icy stuff is served in a parfait glass or sundae dish topped with lightly sweetened whipped cream.

Granita Latte, Granita. Frappuccino (Starbucks). The granitas now popular in the United States are tall blender drinks that combine espresso, milk, sugar, and (usually) vanilla. The best are made fresh on demand in a commercial blender. Icy cold but laced with the perfume of just-brewed espresso, these can be splendid summer drinks. Less successful are granitas produced by dispensing machines, the kind with big see-through tanks filled with various colors of slush. These granitas typically are made with either stale espresso or premade espresso concentrates. They tend to be flat and cloying compared to the fresh-made blender versions.

Chai, Chai Latte. Chai is a drink made with a mix of intensely flavored spices (ginger, cinnamon, cardamom), black tea, and honey or sugar, all mixed in frothed milk and typically served in a tall, latte-sized glass. Although chai is based on traditional recipes from central Asia, the current American version was developed and popularized by the espresso cart culture of the Pacific Northwest. Chai drinks contain no espresso or coffee, but the use of frothed milk as their vehicle most definitely makes them an important component of the new espresso cuisine. To my palate, the best versions of chai are the most traditional, those that combine fresh honey, a liquid concentrate made by boiling actual ground spices, and good black tea. Chai made from "instant chai" mixes can range from decent to absolutely awful: shallow and brassy sweet.

ESPRESSO BREAK

ESPRESSO AND EL GUSTO LATINO

Today the espresso machine is found not only in upscale professional and student and artist hangouts, but in other, less celebrated North American neighborhoods as well.

Cubans, Brazilians, and other Latin American cultures enjoy espresso traditions that may predate the North American—Italian tradition, and wherever Cubans in particular have settled in any numbers they have brought with them their own style of espresso culture.

If you do find Cuban-style espresso being served, much will be familiar: the little white cups half filled with dark coffee, the espresso machine behind the counter. But for Cubans and most Latin Americans, sweet is never sweet enough. Cubans usually pull the espresso directly into a demitasse that may be as much as half filled with sugar. As the hot espresso dribbles into the cup the coffee is stirred, immediately dissolving the sugar. The little cups of sweet black coffee are invariably served backed by glasses of cold water. The coffee itself often displays a particularly smoky, bitter bite.

Such small cups of strong, dark-roasted, filtered coffee have been enjoyed for generations in Latin America, beginning long before the development of espresso technology. In early twentieth-century Cuba, for example, the coffee was brewed by the cold water method. A large amount of dark-roasted, finely ground coffee was steeped in relatively small amounts of cold water for several hours. The resulting concentrated but mild-tasting coffee was then filtered through cotton cloth, stored, and when needed, heated and poured into small cups half filled with sugar. The coffee was always served with glasses of chilled water, seldom if ever mixed with milk, and taken in small quantities often throughout the day, just as Italians today take their espresso.

Before the development of the espresso machine very similar coffee traditions prevailed in Brazil and many other regions of Latin America, although the concentrated coffee was often mixed with hot milk in the morning, and the concentrate itself might be brewed by hot water as well as by cold water methods. In Brazil the brewing water is often sweetened *before* the coffee is brewed by the drip method, and the coffee is served in cups even smaller than the standard demitasse.

Obviously, the espresso method was made to order for such traditions, and it entered the mainstream of many Latin American coffee cultures long before it came into vogue in North America. It wasn't until North Americans discovered the milkier side of the Italian cuisine, the ingratiatingly dessertlike cappuccino and caffè latte, that espresso began its spread into the mainstream of coffee culture in the United States and English-speaking Canada.

THE LATIN TASTE AT HOME

Unless you live in Miami or some other city with a relatively large Cuban community you may not have an opportunity to enjoy the public side of the Latin espresso tradition. However, the Latin taste in espresso can be easily experienced at home.

Simply spoon some sugar—for modest starters, try about a rounded teaspoonful of either refined sugar or demerara (raw sugar)—into a preheated demitasse, and pull the shot directly into the cup and over the sugar, stirring all the while with a demitasse spoon. Cubans also are fond of another sugar overload drink that combines espresso coffee with sweetened, condensed milk. Pour about ½ ounce sweetened, condensed milk in a preheated demitasse and pull a 1¼-ounce shot directly into the milk.

As for the coffee itself, markets in Latin American neighborhoods usually carry a range of excellent preground, packaged espresso coffees in the Latin style. These coffees constitute one of the great uncelebrated pleasures of North American espresso cuisine. They differ both from North American canned espressos, which tend to be lighter in roast and more acidy, and the packaged, preground espressos imported from northern Italy, which are smoother and milder than either Latin or mainstream North American blends. The Latin espresso blends are particularly effective for large, milky drinks like caffè latte, since Italian and mainstream North American packaged espressos may be too mild tasting to power through the milk.

Latin espresso blends usually carry the tag "Para el gusto Latino" ("For the Latin taste") somewhere on the package. They almost always are precision ground for good espresso brewing. The same roaster often offers more than one blend, with a variety of names and packaging. These blends may differ subtly in flavor, but their differences are usually not described in the copy on the bags. A rule of thumb: the darker the colors on the package the longer the coffee has been roasted, and the more characteristically Latin the flavor.

4 FULL CITY TO DARK FRENCH

COFFEE ROASTING AND ESPRESSO

Roasting is one key to the transformation of the tasteless, raw seeds of an obscure tree from the horn of Africa into the rich, resonant beverage we know as coffee. The flavor nuances imparted to coffee by roasting are particularly important in espresso cuisine, because the dark styles of roast used in espresso tend to mute taste characteristics inherent in the bean itself and replace them with characteristics generated by the roast.

ROASTING CHEMISTRY

The green coffee bean, like all the other nuts, kernels, and beans we consume, is composed of fats, proteins, fiber, and miscellaneous chemical compounds. The aroma and flavor that make coffee so distinctive are present only potentially until the heat of roasting simultaneously forces much of the moisture out of the bean and draws out of the base matter of the bean fragrant little beads of a volatile, oily substance variously called *coffee essence, coffee oil,* or *coffeol.* This substance is not properly an oil, since it dissolves in water. It also evaporates easily, quickly absorbs other less desirable flavors, and generally proves to be as fragile a substance as it is tasty. Without it, there's no coffee, only sour brown water and caffeine, yet it constitutes only 0.5 percent of the weight of the bean.

The roasted bean is, in a sense, simply a dry package for this oil. In medium- or American-roast coffee, the oil gathers in little pockets throughout the heart of the bean. As the bean is held in the roaster for longer periods or at higher temperatures, as it is with some darker espresso blends, more moisture is lost, and the oil develops further and begins to rise to the surface of the bean, giving darker-roasted beans their characteristic slick-to-oily appearance. Beneath the oil, the hard matter of the bean begins to contribute the slightly bitter flavor characteristic of the darkest roasts of coffees. Eventually, the bean turns to near charcoal and tastes definitively burned. This ultimately roasted coffee, variously called *dark French, heavy roast, Neapolitan,* or occasionally *Italian,* has an unmistakable charcoal tang.

Dark roasts also contain considerably less acid and somewhat less caffeine than lighter roasts; these substances go up the chimney with the roasting smoke. Consequently, dark roasts used in the espresso cuisine display less of the dry snap or bite coffee people call "acidy" and tend to be sweeter rather than brisk.

ROAST STYLE AND ESPRESSO

The espresso brewing method is so efficient at extracting flavor from coffee that it tends to exaggerate flavor characteristics. Qualities that may be exhilarating or agreeable in other brewing methods can turn into irritating distractions when subject to the amplification of espresso brewing. The espresso method rewards deep, sweet, subtle flavor characteristics rather than those that are extreme or idiosyncratic.

Consequently, the best roasts for espresso brewing are those that are a bit darker than the American norm, but not too dark. Coffees roasted to the light through medium end of the spectrum typically are too acidy and bright, and tend to taste sharp or sour as espresso. On the other hand, extremely dark, almost black roasts come across as thin, watery, and charred.

Roasting Terminology

The common terms for roasts among most coffee sellers are the standard *American* or *medium* roast (medium brown in color; bright and acidy tasting); *Viennese, light French,* or *full city* (slightly darker in color than American; smoother and less acidy with the merest undertone of dark bittersweetness); *Italian, espresso,* or *continental* (medium-dark brown in color with oily patches on the surface of the bean; only the slightest acidy tones, with the bittersweet tang distinct); *Italian, espresso,* or *French* (dark brown in color; surface of the bean covered with oil; all acidy notes gone and the bittersweetness dominant); and *French, dark French,* or *Neapolitan* (nearly black in color; very oily surface; charcoal or burned tones dominate; thin-bodied in the cup).

Of course, the "standard" medium roast varies greatly by region and by roaster. The West Coast traditionally prefers a darker standard than the East Coast, with the Midwest appropriately somewhere between. As for roasters, all vary the roast slightly to bring out what they regard as the unique characteristics of each coffee, but this perfect moment varies according to the philosophy of the roaster. To roasters who adhere to the dark end of the spectrum, lighter-roasted coffees taste too acidy and almost sour; to those who adhere to the light end, darker-roasted coffees taste muted or charred.

Roasting Philosophy and Espresso

A similar difference in philosophy prevails among roasters in regard to espresso coffees. Some prefer to roast their espresso blends less darkly, some more. Some prefer to stop the roasting at the point where the natural sweetness and acidy tones of the coffee are still discernible and the dark-roasted bittersweetness is just beginning to develop, with only patches of oil flecking the still dry surface of the bean. Others prefer a darker roast in which the characteristic bittersweetness of the dark roast completely dominates any remaining acidy tones, and the bean is distinctly dark brown in color and shiny with oil.

It is best to learn to associate flavor with the color and appearance of the bean rather than with name alone, but for reference almost everything you need to know about the names of roasts is condensed in chart form on page 57, with the roast styles used in espresso cuisine indicated.

ONLY BY TASTING

Only by tasting a variety of dark-roasted blends from a variety of coffee roasters can you determine whether you prefer your espresso coffee roasted in a style that leans toward the lighter end of the espresso spectrum, with some of the acidy notes still discernible, or toward the darker end, where the bittersweet tones completely dominate. You may even find that you prefer a distinctly acidy style or (particularly if you liked the coffee you tasted in northern France) a very dark, almost black, charred-tasting style.

Your choice will be complicated because different blends of raw beans respond differently to the impact of the roast. Espresso blends in the classic northern Italian style, like the famous Illy Caffè, combine coffees from Brazil that are naturally sweet, low-acid, and full-bodied. These Brazil beans need only a moderately dark roast to muffle their already mild acidity and develop their inherent sweetness. On the other hand, many West Coast American espresso blends are heavy with powerful, high-grown, brightly acidy beans from Central America that literally need to be tamed by a roast sufficiently dark enough to mute their powerful acidity. For more information on beans and blending see Chapter 5 and Chapter 6.

Furthermore, two dark-roasted coffees may look the same but taste radically different depending on how tactfully the roast was handled. The trick to roasting coffee dark without losing flavor is moderating the temperature inside the roasting chamber toward the end of the roast so the sugars in the bean caramelize rather than burn. Coffees in which the sugars have been burned taste thin, bitter, and carbony, hardly positive characteristics for espresso. If you taste an espresso with those characteristics, try a coffee from a different roasting company.

The best coffee companies roast each component of a blend separately to develop what the roastmaster feels are the optimum qualities that each coffee can bring to the final blend. Consequently, many espresso blends have a mottled look. This is a sign of quality, not of carelessness, particularly when the differences in color among the beans are subtle rather than dramatic.

A drum roaster of the kind often used in smaller specialty coffee-roasting establishments.

ROASTING YOUR OWN

After all of the preceding about how complex properly roasting an espresso coffee can be, the idea of encouraging readers to roast their own espresso coffee at home may seem as misplaced as encouraging someone to climb mountains after showing them a film of the doomed Everest expedition.

However, roasting small batches of coffee at home is much easier than roasting very large quantities of coffee in very large, industrial machines. Think of the difference between cooking for yourself and managing the kitchen for a large restaurant. The small scale of home roasting makes everything much easier. In fact, home coffee roasting probably ranks somewhere between cooking pasta al dente and poaching eggs in order of culinary difficulty.

Home coffee roasting provides the espresso aficionado with several advantages: definitively fresher coffee, less expensive coffee, and above all the opportunity to make unlimited personal experiments with roast and blend.

There are many ways to roast coffee at home. I outline most of them in my book *Home Coffee Roasting: Romance & Revival,* St. Martin's Press. But for the novice, the easiest way to start is to buy a small home coffee roaster that works on the *fluid-bed* principle: the beans are simultaneously heated and agitated by a column of hot air jetting up through the roasting chamber, much like small electric popcorn poppers heat and agitate popping corn.

At this writing three such devices are on the market: the Fresh Roast Coffee Bean Roaster, the Hearthware Precision Coffee Roaster, and the Hearthware Gourmet Coffee Roaster. They retail for $100 to $140. All are simple to use, although they roast a relatively small volume of beans per session. All incorporate a glass roasting chamber, enabling you to observe the changing color of the beans; a chaff collector at the top or back of the roasting chamber to prevent the brown flakes that roasting liberates from coffee beans from blowing around the kitchen; and an adjustable timer, which controls the length of the roast by automatically triggering a cooling cycle. The controls for all three roasters also allow the user to manually override the timer to fine-tune the darkness of the roast, an essential feature.

The only trick with these devices is to learn when to stop the roast to get the darkness of roast and hence the taste you prefer. The longer the green beans roast, the darker the color and the deeper and less bright the taste. Because batches of green coffee beans differ from one another in density and moisture content, it is impossible for the manufacturers (or for me) to specify an exact setting or number of minutes to roast for espresso. Start with the "Dark" setting, taste the result, and fine-tune the setting from there for subsequent batches. With most coffees, there is an optimum moment when the rich bittersweetness that we treasure in espresso peaks, after which the flavor becomes progressively thinner and more burned tasting. This moment comes typically when the beans reach a dark brown, the brown that in furniture stains is called "walnut," and when the roasting smoke smells sweet and full.

The best starting point for fine-tuning the degree of roast is to put a handful of beans roasted to the color you prefer for espresso on the counter next to the machine, start the roast at the maximum dark setting, watch the raw beans through the glass as they gradually roast until they are just *slightly lighter* than your sample beans, then manually override the cooling cycle by advancing the timing dial or by pushing the appropriate button.

With some particularly dense or moist beans you

may need to turn the timing dial *back* to prolong the roast so as to achieve the darkness of roast you favor. One of the three currently available fluid-bed devices, the Fresh Roast, has a switch that slightly increases the heat in the roasting chamber to facilitate achieving darker roasts. When using the Fresh Roast for espresso, start your roasting experiments by placing this switch on the "Dark" setting.

Once you have determined the right length of time to roast a given batch of beans to the style you prefer, you should be able to set the timer and walk away. However, every time you buy a new batch of green beans you probably will need to hover over the roaster once again to determine the appropriate setting. Decaffeinated beans, which start out brown and may roast very quickly, require particularly careful attention.

All home roasting machines come with order forms for green beans. There also are sites on the Internet through which you can order green beans, including very exotic origins. See Sources.

As I indicated earlier, the most careful of espresso roasters roasts each component of a blend separately to best bring out its unique contribution to the total effect of the combined coffees, but for home roasting you may wish to combine the coffees of your blend before roasting. Freshly roasted coffee is at its best if it is allowed to rest for about twenty-four hours after roasting, permitting the recently volatilized oils to stabilize. If you're impatient or needy, however, grind immediately and enjoy.

Common appliances of the nineteenth century: home coffee roasters designed to fit inside the burner of coal or wood stoves.

Final Precautions

Coffee roasting produces smoke. This smoke presents two problems: it can set off smoke alarms if not ventilated, and however pleasant it smells during roasting, it clings and becomes cloying over the long run. Always set up your home roasting machine under the hood of your range and turn on the fan. In clement weather you can roast out of doors on porch or patio.

A second precaution: always use exactly the volume of beans recommended by the manufacturer of your roasting device. Too many or too few beans may not agitate properly and may roast unevenly.

See the following Espresso Break for more on roasting, and Chapters 5 and 6 for more on choosing and blending beans for espresso.

ESPRESSO BREAK
ROAST NAMES AND TASTES

Attaching names to coffee roasts is one of those exercises in communication that are as futile as they are inevitable. Exactly at what point does a drizzle become rain? When does light French roast become Italian roast? One roaster's terminology may be totally different from another's, and in an absolute sense, there are as many shades and nuances of roast as there are batches of coffee that emerge from a roasting machine.

Given that pessimistic introduction, I here present most of the names used in the United States to describe styles of roast, arranged so as to roughly correspond to descriptions of the appearance of the beans and associated taste characteristics. Some names appear in more than one category. Such overlap is necessary because one roaster's French may be another one's Italian. Starbucks has contributed to the confusion by assigning its own publicist-invented names to roast styles. In Starbucks-speak the medium-brown category

is Milder Dimensions, the medium-dark is Lively Impressions, the moderately dark is Rich Traditions, and the dark Bold Expressions.

The highlighted categories all describe roasts suitable for espresso. Choosing from among them is a matter of personal taste. Roasts that are too light for espresso (*light brown* through *medium brown*) produce espresso that tastes sharp and shallow; roasts that are too dark (*very dark brown*) produce a cup that is burned and thin. In general, tall, milky drinks require a darker, more pungent-tasting roast to carry flavor through the milk. Straight espresso, on the other hand, is best produced from blends of naturally sweet beans brought to a relatively moderate roast (*medium-dark brown*).

Also be reminded that the taste of a roast is influenced by the origin or blend of the green beans subject to the roasting (see Chapters 5 and 6), and by the method and handling of the roast.

Roast color	Bean surface	Common names	Comments
Light-medium brown	Dry	**Medium** **Light** **American** Regular	Roasts at the extreme light end of the roast spectrum can taste sour and grainy. Used only for inexpensive commercial blends, never for espresso.
Medium brown	Dry	**Medium** **American** Regular City	The norm for more traditional U.S. specialty roasters, particularly those on the East Coast. Acidy and bright. Never used for espresso cuisine.
Medium-dark brown	Dry to tiny droplets or faint patches of oil	**Viennese** **Full City** **Espresso** **Light French** Light Espresso Continental	The normal, nonespresso roast for most U.S. roasters. Sweeter, rounder, less acidy than lighter roasts. When applied to softer, sweeter coffees, a typical roast for "northern Italian"–style espresso blends intended for straight shots and short milk drinks.
Moderately dark brown	Faint oily patches to entirely shiny surface	**Espresso** French European High Continental	The normal, nonespresso roast for many U.S. West Coast–style specialty roasters. Elsewhere in America, the typical espresso roast. Bittersweet. Carries through a considerable amount of frothed milk.
Dark brown	Shiny surface	**French** **Espresso** **Italian** Dark Turkish	The norm for some U.S. West Coast–style specialty roasters. The typical espresso roast in the western states. Pungent, less sweet than lighter roasts. Carries well through large amounts of frothed milk.
Very dark brown	Very shiny surface	**Italian** **Dark French** Neapolitan Spanish Heavy	The norm for Peet's Coffee & Tea and its imitators. Handled well, as Peet's does, this roast makes a heavy, pungent, but satisfactory espresso. Roasted badly it makes a thin, burned-tasting espresso.
Very dark (nearly black) brown	Shiny surface	**Dark** **French** Spanish Neapolitan	Burned or charcoal-like tones dominate. Thin-bodied. Not a typical roast in the United States unless the roastmaster is careless. Not appropriate for espresso.

5 BOURBON, PARCHMENT, AND MONSOONED MALABAR

A COFFEE BEAN PRIMER FOR ESPRESSO

The relationship between the espresso we drink and the coffee berry as it ripens on a tree on a tropical farm is both simple and complicated. The simple part is obvious: no coffee berry, no espresso. The complex part is everything else. Since the seed of the berry that ultimately becomes espresso is subject to so many complex processes between the moment it ripens and the moment its rich, dark infusion is finally drunk, tracing taste characteristics that appear in the cup back to the bean itself is a perilous undertaking, filled with caveat and equivocation.

Take, for example, a quality embodied by all good espresso: heavy body, meaning a sensation of fullness in the mouth. Starting on the distant, berry end of the process, beans from certain origins definitely do produce a fuller-bodied beverage than do beans from certain other origins. Yet does the full body of a particular demitasse of espresso necessarily mean that the coffees it comprises came from beans known for their heavy body?

Not really. A properly bewed espresso is fuller-bodied than a poorly brewed espresso, for example. Furthermore, coffee roasted either relatively lightly, as in some North American cuisine, or very darkly, as in some northern French cuisine, will produce a lighter-bodied coffee than the middle ranges of dark brown usually used for espresso. Coffees that have been subjected to decaffeination processes frequently display less body than coffees that have not been so processed. Finally, the methods by which the coffee seed has been picked, divested of its fruit, dried, cleaned, and sorted also affects body.

In attempting to make sense of these complexities,

I would like to proceed systematically, first by identifying some broad taste characteristics that apply to coffee generally and espresso coffee in particular, then by describing how various factors and processes that affect the green bean influence those characteristics as they display themselves in the cup of espresso we finally drink.

PROFESSIONAL TASTING CATEGORIES

One of the most desperate acts possible in human communication is attempting to explain how something tastes to someone who hasn't tasted it. Nevertheless, for commercial reasons and because we humans like to talk about experiences that give us pleasure, coffee professionals have come up with some terms for describing the various nuances that manifest in the taste of coffee.

First, here are a few terms and concepts used to discuss the relative merits of various green coffees. These terms describe taste characteristics associated with the bean itself. They reveal themselves most clearly in coffees brought to the relatively light roast used by professionals to "cup" coffee, or evaluate it by taste and smell.

The more romantic of these tasting terms have been carried into the prose used to sell specialty coffees; the less romantic remain the practical property of the folks who actually work in the business.

Acidity, Acidy. Acidity refers to the high, thin notes, the dryness a coffee produces at the back of the palate and under the edges of the tongue. This pleasant tart-

An early twentieth-century cupping room, the gustatory control center of the roasting operation. Note the small roasters on the right back wall, used to roast samples of green coffees, and the rotating tasting table, flanked by hourglass-shaped spittoons (the coffee-cupping ritual involves sucking the coffee noisily from a spoon, swishing it about the mouth, and spitting it out.) Contemporary cupping rooms differ from this one only in detail.

ness, snap, or twist is what coffee people call acidity. In a poor-quality or underroasted coffee the acidy notes can become sour and astringent rather than brisk, but in a fine, medium-roasted arabica coffee, they will be complex, rich, and vibrant. The acidy notes also carry, wrapped in their nuances, much of the distinctiveness of rare coffees.

You will not run into the terms acidity or acidy in your local coffee seller's signs and brochures. Most retailers avoid describing a coffee as acidy for fear consumers will confuse a positive acidy brightness with an unpleasant sourness. Instead you will find a variety of creative substitutes: bright, dry, brisk, vibrant, etc.

The darker the style of roast, the less distinct the

acidy notes will be. In the medium dark brown roasts used in Italian-style espresso cuisine, the acidy notes may continue to reveal themselves, although much less distinctly than in medium roasts. In the dark brown roasts used in most American espresso cuisine, the acidy sensation will have been almost entirely roasted out of the bean.

Body. Body or mouth-feel is the sense of heaviness, richness, and thickness when the coffee is swished around the mouth. To pursue a wine analogy, cabernets and certain other red wines are heavier in body than most white wines. In this case wine and coffee tasters use the same term for a similar sensation, although the chemical basis for the sensation differs between wine and coffee.

Coffees from various parts of the world vary in body. Many celebrated coffees are typically heavy in body; the best Indonesian coffees are particularly so. However, as I indicated earlier, in espresso the roasting and brewing processes have considerably more effect on body than the characteristics of the original green bean. Virtually every detail of advice and prescripiton on espresso brewing offered on pages 141–45 has to do with maximizing body and richness in the final cup.

Aroma. Some coffees may be more aromatic than others, and some may display certain distinctive characteristics more clearly in aroma than in the cup. Typical positive characteristics associated with aroma are subtle floral and fruit tones and vanilla, nut, and vanilla-nut notes.

Again, however, the dark-roasting involved in espresso cuisine mutes such subtleties, partly replacing them with the more general aromatics encouraged by the dark roast, like chocolate and bittersweet notes. Nearly black roasts may display little aroma of any kind except the charcoal pungency of the blackened bean, since virtually all of the delicate aromatic oils will have been burned off.

In the brewing process aroma is particularly promoted by freshness. The more recently the coffee has been roasted and ground, the more powerful the aroma. Once liberated in the cup aroma fades quickly, which is why the little cups used for straight espresso are preheated and the drink consumed quickly.

Finish and Aftertaste. If aroma is the overture of the cup, then finish is the final flourish at the end of the piece and aftertaste the resonant silence thereafter. Both are extremely important characteristics for anyone who genuinely, sensually enjoys coffee. The sensations of a fine coffee perfectly brewed shimmer on our palate in a long, exquisitely fading trajectory, sometimes for an hour or two after we finish the cup. Any weakness or defect in flavor will be similarly and regrettably persistent.

Generally, heavy-bodied coffees have longer and more resonant finishes and display a more persistent aftertaste than lighter-bodied varieties. But once again, in espresso cuisine brewing and roasting may have considerably more impact on finish than the qualities of the bean itself. Freshness in particular affects finish. A freshly roasted and ground espresso coffee will display a much more vibrant finish than coffees that have partly staled.

Flavor. Flavor is the most ambiguous of the tasting categories defined here because it overlaps all of the others. Terms describing positive flavor tones or notes: floral, fruity, vanilla-like, nutty, vanilla-nut-like, chocolaty, caramel, spicy, herby, tobaccoish, pungent. General terms describing flavor include complex, balanced, deep, ordinary, bland, inert, imbalanced, rough. The primary tastes (sweet, salt, sour, bitter) also come into play. Sweetness in particular is a strong modifying influence on other cup characteristics. Natural sweetness is a sign of quality in any coffee, but is a particularly important characteristic for coffees intended for the espresso cuisine. Sweetness indicates that the coffee fruit was picked when ripe and processed with care.

Varietal Distinction. If an unblended coffee has characteristics that set it off from other coffees yet identify it as what it is, it has varietal distinction. A rich, winy-fruit acidity characterizes Yemen and many good East Africa coffees, for example, whereas a low-toned pungency is a distinctive characteristic of most good Sumatra coffees. But, again, the darker roasting in the espresso cuisine mutes most varietal distinctions.

Flavor Defects. These are unpleasant taste sensations created by problems in picking the coffee fruit, removing the fruit from the beans, or drying and storing the beans. Most decent espresso blends are free of flavor defects, but occasionally a coffee sneaks into a blend sufficiently defective to sound a discordant note. The names for defects are numerous, but by the time they emerge in a demitasse of espresso they typically fall into one of two broad categories: ferment, the taste of rotten fruit (caused by the fruit fermenting while in contact with the bean), or hardness or harshness, a sort of aggressive flatness caused by molds or mustiness. Defects sound their unpleasant notes most clearly in aroma and aftertaste.

ESPRESSO TASTING TERMS

The following terms often come up informally in discussions of espresso coffees, though more as terms of connoisseurship than of trade. They relate as much to the effects of brewing and roasting as to the qualities of the original green bean and are less clearly defined than the technical tasting terms defined earlier.

Sweetness. The sensation this term describes is not the brassy monotone of refined white sugar, but rather a vibrant natural sweetness shimmering inside and around other positive sensations. Sweetness in an espresso is owing to inherently sweet beans that have been produced only from ripe fruit, to a tactful roast style that caramelizes the sugars in the bean rather than burning them, and to proper brewing technique.

Bitterness. The bitter bite of some espresso coffees should be distinguished from the acidy tones of a medium-roast coffee, since the bitterness described here is a taste characteristic encouraged by dark roasting. It is not an unpleasant characteristic. Most West Coast American and many Latin American blends are bitter by design. Espresso drinkers in these regions find the lighter-roasted, sweeter espresso blends preferred by northern Italians bland by comparison. If the distinction between bitter and acidy seems abstract, an analogy might help. Acidity is like the dry sensation in most wines, a mild astringency balanced by sweetness. The bitter sensation that arises from dark roasting is more analogous to the bitterness of certain apertifis like Campari, for example; it is a more dominating sensation, and less localized on the palate.

The average North American filter-coffee drinker will call bitter tones "strong," to my mind an inappropriate term. Strong properly refers to the amount of solids and other flavoring agents in the brewed coffee. A dark-roasted coffee could be brewed strong, as it is in the espresso method, or weak, as it might be in a filter-drip system when someone has been stingy with the ground coffee.

Pungency. My word for the pleasant, sweet-yet-twisty tones of a good West Coaast–style American espresso blend. If there is a Peet's coffee store near you, go in and sniff the coffee bins for a suggestion of the sensation I am describing. This aroma complex is seldom encountered in Italian espressos, but is a common characteristic of North- and Latin American blends. It is apparently created by a dark roast achieved slowly. Bitterness might be another word for it.

Smoothness. I take smooth to be an epithet describing an espresso coffee that can be taken comfortably without milk and with very little sugar, a coffee in which a heavy body and the sweet sensation described above predominate over bitter and acidy tones.

WHAT MAKES GREEN BEANS DIFFERENT

If green coffee beans embody differing taste characteristics, what causes these differences? The following pages describe factors influencing coffee quality and flavor in the green bean before it has been subjected to subsequent processes like blending, roasting, decaffeination, and brewing.

Botany
Species. All of the world's finest coffees, and some that are not so fine, belong to the species *Coffea arabica,* the species that first hooked the world on coffee. Second in commercial importance among coffee species is *Coffea canephora* or robusta, a lower-growing, more disease-resistant, heavier-bearing species of the coffee tree. Robusta produces a bean that is rounder in shape than the arabica bean, blander in flavor, heavier in body, somewhat heavier in caffeine content, and cheaper than most Arabica. Coffee from the robusta species is widely used in cheaper commercial canned blends and instant or soluble coffees, but has little importance in the world of fancy single-origin coffees. High-quality robustas may be used in small quantities in some Italian espresso blends because of their heavy body. Others of the hundreds of known coffee species, particularly *Coffea liberica,* are grown commercially, but are not important in the larger pic-

ture. What have become important are some recently developed, controversial hybrid varieties of *Coffea arabica,* such as *var. catimor,* that include some robusta in their parentage.

Variety. Just as there are McIntosh apples and Golden Delicious apples, Cabernet wine grapes and Merlot wine grapes, there are various botanical *varieties* or *cultivars* of *Coffea arabica.* Some of these varieties are long established and traditional, the kind of varieties that gardeners call heirloom. They are the product of happy coincidence, of a process of spontaneous mutation and human selection that may have taken place decades, sometimes centuries, ago. These heirloom varieties, or *old Arabicas* as they are called in the coffee world, include *var. typica,* the original variety cultivated in Latin America; the famous *var. bourbon,* which first appeared on the Island of Reunion (then Bourbon) in the Indian Ocean in the eighteenth century; the odd and rapidly disappearing *var. maragogipe* (Mah-rah-go-ZHEE-pay), which produces a very large, porous bean and first appeared in Maragogipe, Brazil. In addition, there are many noble varieties that are grown only in the regions where they first appeared. These locally based varieties include the *var. lintong,* which produces the finest coffees of Sumatra; the Ismaili and Mattari cultivars of Yemen; and the almost vanished *var. old chick* of India.

Coffees from such traditional varieties are particularly valued in the fancy coffee world. In recent years green-revolution scientists working in growing countries have produced varieties of arabica that are more disease-resistant, heavier-bearing, and faster to reach maturity than the older, traditional varieties. Two of the most controversial of these so-called *new Arabicas* are the *Colombiana* or *Colombia* (developed and widely planted in Colombia) and the sinister-sounding *Ruiru 11* (Kenya).

Coffee professionals in the United States are almost unanimous in condemning all such new hybrid varieties for lacking the complexity and nuance of their beloved old arabicas. However, the flavor issue is much more complex than many coffee professionals would have us believe. There is no doubt that coffee from different varieties tastes different, even when the trees are grown on the same soil under the same conditions. But are the old arabicas always better tasting than the new? Not consistently. Cup quality seems to depend on a complex, often unpredictable interaction of variety and local growing conditions. The classic Typica variety that produces the celebrated Kona coffees of Hawaii has turned out to be a taste bust when planted on other Hawaiian islands under different growing conditions from Kona. Bourbon, the traditional premium variety of Brazil, seems consistently more complex and interesting in the cup than newer varieties when grown in Brazil. But will seeds of those Bourbon trees, in growing situations other than Brazil, necessarily produce coffee with similar superiority? Perhaps. Perhaps not. I recently organized a blind tasting of El Salvador coffees in which a relatively recently developed hybrid called Pacamara scored better than a Bourbon from the same farm.

The situation is further complicated by the existence of varieties that, like the old arabicas, are spontaneous mutants, but which did their mutating at a relatively recent date in history. They include the widely planted *var. caturra* (1935) and *var. mundo novo* and *var. Kent.*

By now my point should be clear: there are no big, simple answers in respect to variety, only little answers and passionately held positions. Interested aficionados can only stay tuned.

Altitude

The arabica species grows best at altitudes ranging from around 1,500 to 6,000 feet. Generally, the higher grown the coffee the more slowly the seed, or bean, develops, and the harder and denser the bean. Such high-grown or hard-bean coffees are valued in the fancy coffee market because generally they display a heavier body, a more complex flavor, and a more pronounced and vibrant acidity than lower-grown coffees.

However, these high-grown, acidy coffees are a bit overbearing for many people's palates, and they most definitely do not make the best espressos. The espresso brewing system produces a highly concentrated coffee that intensifies certain taste characteristics like acidity. For this reason powerfully acidy coffees may be too sharp for espresso blends and can imbalance the cup. Some of the most sought-after coffees for espresso blending are lower-grown, sweeter coffees like the best coffees of Brazil.

Picking, Processing, and Drying

The care with which coffee is picked, the manner in which the fruit is removed from the bean, and the way in which the bean is dried after removal of the fruit all profoundly affect coffee taste and quality.

Picking and Sorting the Fruit. Coffee fruit does not ripen uniformly. Both ripe and unripe berries, or *cherries* as they are called in the coffee trade, typically festoon the same branch. The best coffees are hand-picked as they ripen. Cheaper coffees are stripped from the trees in a single operation, thus combining ripe, unripe, and overripe berries, not to mention leaves, twigs, and dirt, in the same batch. Somewhere between selective handpicking and strip picking is machine picking, in which rods vibrate the tree branches just enough to cause ripe cherries to drop off the tree. Growers often try to compensate for machine or strip picking by careful mechanical separation of ripe cherries from less ripe and overripe. Although such post-picking sorting can partly compensate for failures in picking, the sweetest and finest coffees continue to be produced from cherries that have been selectively handpicked.

Removing the Fruit from the Bean. Common wisdom in the coffee trade declares that wet processing, in which the outer layers of the coffee fruit are carefully removed from the seed or bean in a complex set of operations before the bean is dried, produces the best coffee. The same wisdom declares that dry-processed or natural coffee, in which the fruit and skin are allowed to shrivel and dry around the bean, then later removed by abrasion, is inferior to such wet-processed or washed coffee. This generalization overlooks the fact that many of the world's most interesting coffees are either dry-processed (Yemen mocha for example), or processed in a way that combines wet- and dry-processing (most Sumatra coffees).

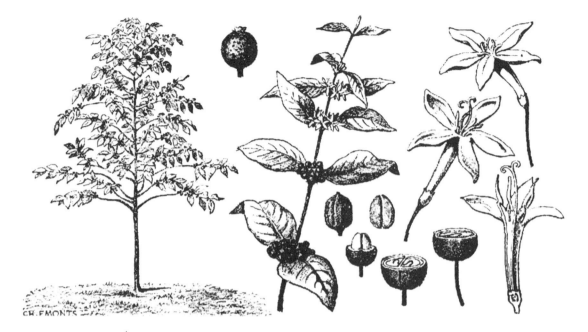

At the left a coffee tree; in the center a coffee branch, with flowers near the top of the branch modulating to ripe fruit near the bottom. At right are representations of the coffee flower, which is white in color, and below that illustrations showing how the coffee seed or bean is nestled inside the coffee fruit.

What really counts is the care taken in processing the coffee, regardless of method. Many dry-processed coffees are also strip picked and carelessly handled, which means that overripe, rotting fruit and other vegetable matter (not to mention whatever animal matter happens to be on the ground at the time) may be piled together during the drying process, tainting the flavor of the entire batch. Such practices have given dry-processing an undeservedly bad reputation.

In fact, coffee that has been dry-processed with care often makes the best espresso. Good dry-processed coffees often display a sweeter, deeper, more complex flavor than the cleaner but more transparent taste of wet-processed coffees, probably owing to the effect of the fruit drying around the bean. Italian roasters almost unanimously prefer dry-processed Brazil coffees for their espresso blends.

Cleaning and Sorting the Beans. In general, the more care taken in removing various unwanted material—stones, twigs, discolored or immature beans, and the like—from the sound coffee beans, the cleaner and fuller the flavor of the coffee will be and the higher price it will command. The cleaning and sorting process can be done by machine, by hand, or by some combination of both.

Grading. Grading is a process that assigns value to coffees for purposes of trading. It ultimately is a kind of sophisticated sorting that divides a given growing region's coffee production into categories according to various quality-related criteria. These criteria vary from country to country, but typically include number of defects (including everything from broken or misshapen beans to sticks), size of the bean (bigger is usually better because bigger beans come from riper fruit), growing altitude (higher is usually better), method of processing (wet vs. dry), and cup quality.

Age of the Beans

Coffees that are roasted and sold soon after processing are called *new crop* and generally display more acidity, brighter, clearer flavor notes, and a thinner body than *old crop* coffees, which have been held in warehouses for a year or two before roasting; *mature* coffees, which have been held for two to three years; or *vintage* or *aged* coffees, which have been held for several years. The longer coffees are held, the heavier their body and the more muted their acidity becomes, until, in aged or vintage coffees, the acidity and other subtle aromatics disappear altogether to be replaced by a rather static heaviness. Unfortunately, many aged coffees now sold in the United States seem to display a hard taste along with the desirable heaviness, perhaps owing to contact with excessive moisture during

aging. Aged coffees are sometimes used in premium espresso blends to balance younger, brighter coffees.

Monsooned Malabar is a special kind of coffee produced in India by exposing dry-processed arabica coffees to monsoon winds in open warehouses. The ambient moisture seems to partly replace the original moisture in the bean, producing a coffee that is mono-toned, pungent, and heavy-bodied. Some espresso blenders use Monsooned Malabar to anchor the bottom notes of their blends.

Soil, Climate, and Other Geographic Intangibles

Certain coffees are world famous: Jamaica Blue Mountain, for example, and Hawaii Kona. Others should be, such as Ethiopia Yirgacheffe and the best Kenya coffees. Such coffees, which are grown in certain limited geographical areas, may display distinct flavor characteristics that coffee fanciers admire. Yirgacheffe is light-bodied, flowery, and fruity; the best Kenya AA displays a deeply dimensioned acidity alive with winelike and berry notes.

Such differences in flavor characteristics are undoubtedly owing to a combination of factors, including botanical species and variety, altitude, and method of picking and processing. Clearly, however, local climate and soil are primary determining factors in determining regional flavor characteristics.

There are even more elusive environmental influences on coffee taste than those determined by region: east-facing slopes versus west-facing slopes, for example; subtle local variations in rainfall; local differences in soil composition. I have tasted coffees from farms in the Kona district of Hawaii that were dramatically different in cup characteristics from coffees grown on farms at the same altitude only a half mile away.

Such distinctions are wonderfully interesting (if baffling) but are less important in the world of espresso than the world of fine coffees intended for drip brewing. Nevertheless, some of the unique flavor notes of the world's most distinctive coffees are integrated into the finest espresso blends, stretching the range and complicating the final flavor profile.

BLENDS AND BLENDING

Blends can combine coffees brought to different degrees of roast, coffees with different caffeine contents, and/or straight coffees from different origins.

For example, roasters frequently blend darker and lighter roasts to produce a more complex flavor than can be obtained with coffees brought to the same degree of roast. Blending also is used to modulate caffeine content: caffeine-free and ordinary beans are often combined in varying proportions to produce blends with half the caffeine in ordinary coffee, or two-thirds, or one-third, etc.

Much more common, however, and more challenging, is blending coffees of approximately the same caffeine content and roast, but from different origins. As practiced in the supermarket canned and instant coffee business, such blending aims to keep costs as low as possible while maintaining a consistent, if lackluster, flavor profile. Specialty or fancy coffee roasters also may blend for price, but with less urgency and

compromise. The overriding goal of specialty blenders is simply producing a coffee that is more complete and pleasing in its totality than any of its unblended components would be alone. This goal is particularly important in espresso, because the concentrated cup produced by the espresso brewing method tends to reward balance and completeness rather than the often interesting but imbalanced flavor profiles of coffees from single origins.

Complete and Pleasing?

In the case of an espresso blend, what constitutes "more complete and pleasing" is obviously relative: relative to the palate of the blender, to the expectations of the consumer, and to the traditions to which both blender and consumer refer.

At this point it might be useful to refer to the array of tasting terms listed earlier: acidity, body, aroma, finish, sweetness, bitterness, and so on.

It would be safe to say that all espresso blends everywhere aspire to as full a body as possible, as much sweet sensation as possible, and as much aroma and as long and resonant a finish as possible. The differences arise with acidity and with the bitter side of the bittersweet taste equation.

Most northern Italian roasters present blends with almost no acidy notes whatsoever, whereas North American espresso blends often maintain some of the dry, acidy undertones most Americans and Canadians are accustomed to in their lighter-roasted coffees. This difference is simply a matter of choice and tradition. North Americans are used to acidy, high-grown

Latin American coffees, and Italians are accustomed to drinking either African robustas or lower-altitude Brazil arabicas.

My own position, for what it's worth, is that acidy notes need to be felt but not tasted in espresso blends. They should be barely discernible, yet vibrating in the heart of the blend.

Recall that acidity, or dryness, is a property of the bean that diminishes as the roast becomes darker, to eventually be replaced entirely by the bittersweet, pungent flavor notes characteristic of dark roasts. The value of the bitter side of the bittersweet equation is also an issue in blending philosophy, with Italian and Italian-style roasters coming down more on the sweet side, and North American roasters more on the bittersweet. As I pointed out in discussing style of roast, this difference is reflected in the somewhat lighter roasts preferred by Italian roasters, opposed to the darker styles favored by most North American roasters.

So, on both accounts, blending philosophy and style of roast, northern Italians put a premium on sweetness and smoothness and North Americans on punch.

It is clear why North Americans might prefer a punchier, more pungent and more acidy espresso coffee: They need the power of such flavor notes to carry through all of the milk they tend to add to their lattes and cappuccinos. Italians generally take their espresso undiluted and so might logically prefer a smoother, sweeter blend. But such an explanation may be entirely too rational. After all, those purist Italians also tend to dump large quantities of sugar into their smooth, sweet espresso blends. Probably taste in espresso blends is simply another irrationality of culture and tradition.

Achieving Blending Goals

At any rate, if heavy body, seductive aroma, a muted acidty, and (in the case of American-style espresso blends) sweet-toned pungency are the goals, how does one attempt to achieve these goals in blending?

In general, roasters choose one or more coffees that provide a base for a blend, additional *highlight coffees* that contribute brightness, energy, and nuance, and (often but not always) bottom-note coffees that intensify sensations of body weight.

Base Coffees. Coffees that provide the base for espresso blends should not be neutral, at least not in my view. They definitely should not be dull or bland. They should be agreeable, without distracting idiosyncrasy or overly aggressive acidity, round and sweet, and they should take a dark roast well. The classic base for espresso is Brazil coffees that have been dry-processed, or dried inside the fruit, a practice that promotes sweetness and body. Peru and some Mexico coffees (all of which are wet-processed) also make a gentle but lively base for espresso. Coffees from the Indonesian island of Sumatra are favorite base coffees among many West Coast–style American blenders. Like Brazils, Sumatras are low-keyed, rather full-bodied coffees, but brought to a dark roast they tend to be bittersweet and pungent, qualities suited to the dark-roasted, sharp, milk-mastering blends favored caffè-latte-happy West Coasters.

Highlight Coffees. These may be any coffee with character, energy, and power. Kenya, with its resonant dimension and winelike acidity, is a favorite highlight coffee among American blenders. Other blenders may prefer the round, clean power of good Costa Ricas, the twistier, often fruit-toned energy of Guatemala Antiguas, or the singing, floral sweetness of washed Ethiopias.

Bottom-Note Coffees and the Robustas Controversy. Blenders often add coffees whose primary contribution to the cup is weight and character. Bottom-note coffees are particularly important in espresso, where resonance and body are paramount. Sumatra Mandhelings are sometimes used as bottom-note coffees, as are specially handled coffees like India Monsooned Malabar and aged coffees. The most controversial bottom-note coffees are the heavy but inert coffees of the robusta species. Italian blenders use robustas freely in their espresso blends to promote body and the formation of crema, the golden froth that covers the surface of a well-made tazzina of espresso. North American blenders use robustas in their espresso blends very sparingly, if at all. I have waffled about the value of robustas in espresso blends over the years, but at this moment I am a robusta naysayer. To my palate robustas are simply too dull and lifeless. They may contribute body, but in return they tend to suck life out of a blend, absorbing nuance and deadening the profile.

CAUSE COFFEES: FOR EARTH, BIRDS, AND PEOPLE

In recent years an expanding array of environmentally friendly, socially progressive, migratory bird–friendly, variously issue-oriented coffees have stepped forward to make their case to right-minded coffee lovers. These cause coffees are less prominent in the world of espresso than in the world of fancy single-origin coffees, probably because the focus in espresso is more on the drama of the drink and less on the coffee itself.

Nevertheless, espresso drinkers can be as concerned as anyone else about health, environment, and social issues, so here is a much condensed list of issue coffees and their related causes and controversies. For a more thorough discussion of these coffee categories and the issues animating them, consult the companion volume to this one, *Coffee: A Guide to Buying, Brewing, & Enjoying.*

Organically Grown Coffees. The granddaddy of environmentally correct coffees, "organics" are certified by independent agencies to have been grown and processed without use of synthetic fertilizers, pesticides, herbicides, or fungicides. Organic growing methods usually produce less coffee per acre, and lower yields plus the cost of certification mean growers face higher costs, which translate to higher retail prices for organically grown coffees. Is the extra cost worth it?

The health benefits of organic coffees for consumers are probably minor. Remember that we don't eat the fruit of the coffee tree as we do the fruit of an apple tree. Instead we use only the seed of the fruit, which is dried, roasted at very high temperatures, and infused in hot water. Then we throw the remnants of the seed away and drink the water. Thus, it would seem that eating organic apples or carrots is far more important to our health than drinking organic coffee.

Furthermore, many coffees are de facto organic because the peasant growers have never been able to afford chemicals in the first place. To cite three well-known examples, it is unlikely that most Yemen, Ethiopia, or Sumatra coffees have been anywhere near expensive manufactured agricultural poisons or supplements.

However, it also is certain that, on the growing end of things, organic growing procedures are of enormous benefit: to air, to earth, to animals, to people. It is more for environmental and social reasons that many coffee lovers are willing to spend a penny or two more per cup for a certified organically grown coffee.

Shade-Grown Coffees. In many places in the world coffee is traditionally grown under a canopy of shade trees. *Coffea arabica* orginally grew wild in the shade of the mountain forests of central Ethiopia, and in many (but not all) coffee-growing regions of the world shade has proven to be essential in protecting coffee from the parching effect of the tropical sun. Recently, studies have begun to show the importance of these shade canopies to everything from sheltering migrating birds to slowing global warming. But just as the awareness of the importance of coffee shade canopies is sinking in, shade-growing fields in many parts of the world are being rapidly replaced by fields of hybrid coffee varieties that grow well in full sun.

These two developments—on one hand, the understanding of how important shade-coffee canopies are to the environment; on the other, the trend toward growing coffee in full sun—has led to marketing of *shade-grown* and *bird-friendly* coffees. Audubon Society chapters have been particularly active in supporting shade-grown coffees that offer crucial shelter to songbirds on their migrations through Central and South American coffee-growing countries.

The bureaucratic machinery necessary for defining and certifying "shade-grown" coffee is in the process of development. Currently the Smithsonian Institution licenses certified organic coffees that *also* meet Smithsonian criteria for growth under a biodiverse shade canopy. Such ultimately environmentally correct coffees are permitted to use the Smithsonian Migratory Bird Center's "Bird Friendly" trademark. Until additional clear certification procedures are in place, bird lovers (not to mention oxygen lovers) will have to take the word of the seller that other, non-certified-organic coffees are indeed shade-grown.

The entire idea of certifying shade-grown coffee is wildly controversial among some coffee growers and exporters because in many parts of the world coffee is traditionally *not* grown in shade. These traditional full-sun growing regions are often so wet and humid that the coffee trees need full sun, or so far from the equator that trees grown in shade become leggy. The world's first commercial coffee, Yemen mocha, has been grown in full sun for four hundred years. Other traditional sun-grown coffees include Hawaii Kona,

Jamaica Blue Mountain, Sumatra Mandheling, and all Brazil coffees. Critics of shade-grown certification argue that the real target should be those growers who *switch* from shade to sun, not those who have grown their coffee in full sun for generations.

Fair-Traded and Other Socially Responsible Coffees. The majority of the world's coffee is grown by peasant farmers on small plots. Few of these farmers receive anything close to a decent price for their coffee, while fine coffee itself remains a dramatically underpriced beverage. The world's most expensive coffee, brewed at home, costs less per ounce than Coca-Cola.

From that preamble readers may suspect that I am a supporter of any system that helps return some of the money we pay for coffee back to the peasant growers who, essentially, suffer grinding poverty so that relatively wealthy Americans can pay a few cents less per pound for an already underpriced luxury.

A *Fair Trade Certified* seal on a coffee means that growers, usually small peasant growers, have been paid a reasonable, formula-defined price for their coffee. The fair-trade movement is quite prominent in Europe, less so in the free-trading, price-busting United States. More typical in the United States are arrangements between individual roasters and groups of peasant growers that return a percentage of the retail price of a coffee directly back to the growers to support development projects ranging from clinics and schools to new roads and mills. Such arrangements are well advertised by the roasters who sponsor them, and often extend to coffees suitable for espresso cuisine.

Sustainable Coffees. Readers may wonder why all of these environmentally and socially concerned coffee folk don't join together in common cause. After all, aficionados who seek quality have a lot in common with the birders who support shade-grown coffee, since the traditional varieties of arabica that aficonados admire are often grown in shade, while the despised new hybrids are typically grown in full sun.

Just such a big-tent approach to conscience coffees is underway. It's called the sustainable coffee movement, and tries to bring together everyone from cranky connoisseurs to birders, health fanatics, and social progressives.

One, perhaps limited, version of the sustainable vision has been advanced by the Rainforest Alliance, whose *eco-OK* seal certifies that Eco-OK inspectors have found that qualifying coffee farms and mills meet a wide variety of environmental criteria, including wildlife diversity, nonpolluting practices, and responsible and limited use of agrochemicals, as well as social and economic criteria that support the welfare of farmers and workers.

Unfortunately, the current sustainable movement offends some supporters of organically grown coffees, who feel that the sustainable idea is a warm, fuzzy rip-off that dilutes everything they have worked for. It also bothers quality-oriented purists, who feel that the only criteria for selling coffee should be how good the coffee tastes in the cup. Time will tell whether the inclusive goals of the sustainable movement can be turned into a practical system with clear and verifiable criteria satisfactory to its many passionate voices and communities.

ESPRESSO BREAK

DECAFFEINATED COFFEES

The Garden without the Snake

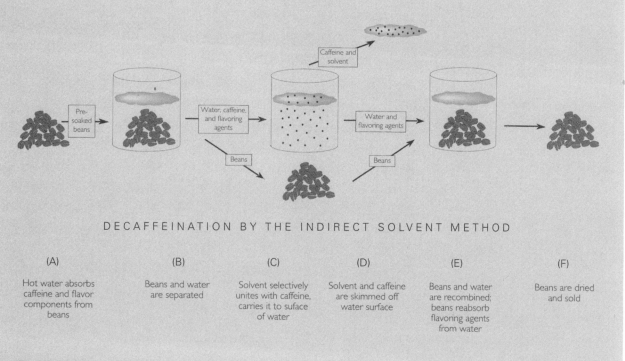

DECAFFEINATION BY THE INDIRECT SOLVENT METHOD

(A)	(B)	(C)	(D)	(E)	(F)
Hot water absorbs caffeine and flavor components from beans	Beans and water are separated	Solvent selectively unites with caffeine, carries it to suface of water	Solvent and caffeine are skimmed off water surface	Beans and water are recombined; beans reabsorb flavoring agents from water	Beans are dried and sold

Decaffeinated, or caffeine-free, coffees have had the caffeine soaked out of them. Most specialty roasters offer a variety of decaffeinated dark-roast coffees suitable for espresso cuisine.

Coffee is decaffeinated in its green state, before the delicate oils are developed through roasting. Hundreds of patents exist for decaffeination processes, but only a few are actually used.

The trick, of course, is how to take out the caffeine without also removing the various components that give coffee its complex flavor.

TRADITIONAL OR EUROPEAN PROCESS

In the process variously called the *solvent process, European process, traditional process,* or *conventional process,* that trick is accomplished through the use of a solvent that selectively unites with the caffeine. There are two variants to the solvent approach.

The *direct solvent process* opens the pores of the beans by steaming them and applies the solvent directly to the beans before removing both solvent and caffeine by further steaming.

The *indirect solvent process* first removes virtually everything, including the caffeine, from the beans by soaking them in hot water (in the diagram on page 75), then separates the beans and water and strips the caffeine from the flavor-laden water by means of the caffeine-attracting solvent. The solvent-laden caffeine is then skimmed from the surface of the water, and the water, now free of both caffeine and solvent, is reunited with the beans, which soak up the flavor components again. The beans are then dried and sold.

With both direct and indirect solvent methods the caffeine is salvaged and sold to makers of pharmaceuticals and soft drinks.

Solvents currently in use are methylene chloride and ethyl acetate. Neither has been fingered as a health threat by the medical establishment, although methylene chloride has been implicated in the depletion of the ozone layer. Ethyl acetate is found naturally in fruit, so you may see coffees decaffeinated by processes making use of it called *natural process* or *naturally* decaffeinated.

Note that both methylene chloride and ethyl acetate evaporate very easily. Even if small amounts of solvent remain in the beans, it is highly unlikely that significant residues survive the high temperatures of the roasting and brewing processes that occur before the coffee is actually drunk. Nevertheless, consumers' almost metaphysical fear of

such substances has led to the commercial development of alternative processes.

SWISS-WATER OR WATER-ONLY PROCESS

There are two phases to this commercially successful process. In the first, start-up phase (see the diagram on page 77), green beans are soaked in hot water, which removes both flavor components and caffeine from the beans. This first, start-up batch of beans is then discarded, while the caffeine is stripped from the water by means of activated charcoal filters, leaving the flavor components behind in the water and producing what the Swiss-Water Process people call "flavor-charged water"—water crammed full of the goodies but without the caffeine. This special water becomes the medium for the decaffeination of subsequent batches of green beans.

When soaked in the flavor-charged but caffeine-free water, new batches of beans give up their caffeine but not their flavor components, which remain more or less intact in the bean. Apparently the water is so charged with flavor components that it can absorb no more of them, whereas it *can* absorb the villainous caffeine.

Having thus been deprived of their caffeine but not their flavor components, the beans are then dried and ready for sale, while the flavor-charged water is cleaned of its caffeine by another run through charcoal filters and sent back to decaffeinate a further batch of beans.

The problem with this process for specialty coffee roasters is the fact that the flavor components of various batches of beans

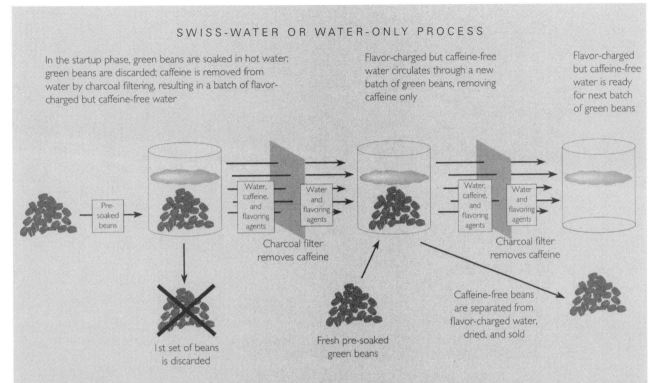

In the startup phase, green beans are soaked in hot water; green beans are discarded; caffeine is removed from water by charcoal filtering, resulting in a batch of flavor-charged but caffeine-free water

Flavor-charged but caffeine-free water circulates through a new batch of green beans, removing caffeine only

Flavor-charged but caffeine-free water is ready for next batch of green beans

Pre-soaked beans

Water, caffeine, and flavoring agents

Water and flavoring agents

Charcoal filter removes caffeine

Water, caffeine, and flavoring agents

Water and flavoring agents

Charcoal filter removes caffeine

1st set of beans is discarded

Fresh pre-soaked green beans

Caffeine-free beans are separated from flavor-charged water, dried, and sold

may become a bit blurred. If your coffee is an Ethiopia, for example, and yesterday's batch was a Colombia, it may be hard to determine exactly whose flavor components actually inhabit the bean at the end of the process. Your Ethiopia may end up with a little of yesterday's Colombia in it, whereas tomorrow's Costa Rica may end up with a little of your Ethiopia, and so on.

The Swiss-Water people have various ways of correcting for this problem, however, and over the years have steadily improved the quality of their product. This success, combined with the encouraging fact that no solvent whatsoever is used in the process and the reassuring ring of "Swiss-Water," with its associations of glaciers, alpine health enthusiasts, and

chewy breakfast cereal, have combined to make this process the most popular of the competing decaffeination methods among specialty coffee consumers.

CARBON DIOXIDE OR CO₂ PROCESS

In this method, the green beans are bathed in highly compressed carbon dioxide (CO_2), the same naturally occurring substance that plants consume and human beings produce. In its compressed form the carbon dioxide behaves partly like a gas and partly like a liquid, and has the property of combining selectively with caffeine. The caffeine is stripped from the CO_2 by means of activated charcoal filters.

CAFFEINE, FLAVOR, AND DECAFFEINATION PROCESSES

Since caffeine in itself is tasteless, coffee flavor should not be affected by its removal. However, in the process of its removal, coffee beans are subjected to considerable abuse, including (depending on the process) prolonged steaming and exposure to solvent or soaking in hot water and/or liquid CO_2. Consequently, most caffeine-free coffees are difficult to roast, and in general display somewhat less body and aroma than similar untreated coffees. You can, of course, create blends of treated and untreated beans, thus cutting down on caffeine intake while maintaining full flavor and body in at least one component of the blend.

6 BLENDS, ROASTS, AND ORIGINS

BUYING ESPRESSO COFFEE

Choosing a coffee is one of the delightful challenges of home espresso brewing. Although the subtlest of distinctions among single-origin coffees are lost in dark-roasting, the rich diversity of the espresso-suitable coffees now available presents the espresso drinker with a fascinating arena for experiment and connoisseurship.

CANS, PODS, BAGS, AND BULK

Coffees suitable for espresso brewing can be purchased in four forms: pre-ground in cans; as pre-ground, pre-packed single servings called "pods"; whole beans in cans and bags; and whole beans in bulk.

Buying whole beans in bags or bulk offers the espresso drinker by far the greatest number of blends and single-origin coffees from which to choose. For the true aficionado, there also is the alternative of buying coffee green and roasting it at home. Home roasters can assemble a veritable cellar of fine coffees, since in its green state coffee keeps rather well. Enough instruction to get started roasting at home is given on pages 53–56.

Pre-Ground, Canned Blends

Pre-ground coffees sold in supermarket cans are almost always blends. The only exception I'm aware of at this writing is a canned dark-roast Colombia.

Many of the most widely distributed canned dark-roast coffees are ground far too coarsely for home espresso brewing. If you are a novice trying home espresso brewing for the first time, do *not* start with a canned dark-roast coffee ground for all-purpose brewing. The coarse grind will only lead to watery, underextracted coffee and frustration. Several packaged dark-roast coffees *are* ground to espresso specifications, however. The labels of these true espresso coffees usually display language like "ground extra-fine for espresso brewing."

In style, pre-ground, canned espresso blends range from mild, sweet styles prepared in northern Italy to reflect classic Italian taste, like the famous Illy Caffè, to much more darkly-roasted coffees with an earthy twist intended for "the Latin taste," as the language on the can usually puts it, to a 100 percent Colombian with dry, acidy notes vibrating inside the bittersweetness of the dark-roast flavor. These canned, pre-ground coffees can provide a helpful orientation to the range of experience possible in espresso-style blends.

Nevertheless, canned coffees are limited in several respects. First of all, pre-ground coffees, regardless of packaging, simply cannot deliver a cup of espresso as fresh as can recently roasted whole-bean coffees ground immediately before brewing. Secondly, canned coffees can't come close to offering the espresso aficionado the variety that whole-bean coffees do.

Espresso Pods

Pods are small, tea bag–like paper sacks of ground, blended espresso intended to fit into special filters provided with many pump espresso machines. They are typically packaged in single-serving foil envelopes. You open the envelope, pop the pod into the filter, and brew. The pod comes out of the filter as cleanly and simply as it went in.

Pods offer clear reassurance for the beginner because they are easy to use and guarantee a proper dose of properly ground coffee. However, they are very expensive, offer limited choice of coffee, and can only be used with pod-compatible pump machines (category 3, pages 107–11). Furthermore, they create a good deal more waste packaging than whole-bean coffees.

Some pods are proprietary in format and designed to work with only one brand of machine, and vice versa. Increasingly, however, home pump machines are designed to give users the option of using either regular ground coffee *or* generic pods that work with any machine which follows something called the ESE (Easy Serving Espresso) standard. I strongly recommend that those interested in brewing with pods opt for maximum flexibility by buying one of the pod-optional, ESE generic-format machines rather than a machine that uses a proprietary pod format. Pod users almost always graduate to regular coffee when two points become apparent to them: first, brewing espresso is not so hard after all, and second, by using pods they are paying too much for less than fresh coffee.

Pods, like canned espresso coffees, are almost always blends. Like canned blends, pod blends usually come in a range of styles, from mild northern Italian styles to dark, pungent blends suitable for large milk drinks like caffè latte. Pods offer slightly more choice in coffee than do canned blends, but again, not nearly as much choice as whole bean.

Buying Whole-Bean Coffees for Espresso

Buying coffee as whole beans and grinding them just before brewing is by far the best alternative for espresso drinkers who are serious about quality. Buying whole-bean coffees and having them ground at the store is probably second-best.

Whole-bean coffees offer much more choice for espresso brewing, and produce (in most cases) a fresher, richer, more fragrant beverage.

Whole-bean coffees are sold in two forms: fresh in bulk from bins and in foil valve bags. The valve bags are designed to protect the coffee from both moisture and oxygen, the two sources of staling in coffee. The oxygen is usually flushed from the bags by using an inert gas like nitrogen before the freshly roasted coffee is dropped into the bag and the bag sealed. Freshly roasted coffee produces carbon dioxide, which is trapped inside the bag, further protecting the coffee from oxygen. The valve imbedded in the bag allows excess carbon dioxide to escape and prevents the bag from inflating.

Such bags most definitely do protect coffee from staling, but for how long? Not over a month, in my experience. But less responsible roasters and stores keep foil bags of coffee around for two, sometimes even three, months. One firm headquartered in Hawaii prints a "best by" date on the bottom of its bags *one year* from the roast date.

Furthermore, simply because a coffee is sold in bulk from a bin doesn't mean it's freshly roasted. Starbucks, for example, packages all of its bulk coffees in valve bags. Clerks simply open the bags and dump the coffee into the bins.

The bottom line? Freshly roasted coffee sold within a week of roasting is best. Freshly roasted coffee held in valve bags are a close second if the bags not held for more than three or four weeks.

Unfortunately, few retailers roast-date their coffee. They code the bags so that employees who stock the shelves know how old a coffee is, but customers don't.

Ultimately, whether the coffee appears in bags or bins, it comes down to trusting your taste buds and trusting the store. Specialized coffee stores with high volumes are almost always more reliable sources than supermarkets. Stores with high volumes are typically more trustworthy than new stores with low volumes. Stores that roast on premises can be the best place of all to buy whole-bean coffees, assuming the roasting is done right. Locations of specialty coffee stores can usually be found in telephone classified pages under the retail coffee heading.

Stores of very large specialty coffee chains like Starbucks, Timothy's World Coffee, Peet's Coffee & Tea, and others offer a sort of compromise between locally run specialty stores and the supermarket. These companies may roast their coffee in very large quantities at centralized locations, but they put a laudable and largely successful emphasis on delivering fresh coffee. How the great-expanding-coffee-chain story will play out eventually in terms of freshness and quality remains to be seen.

Starbucks' current excursion onto the shelves of supermarkets appears less laudable and less successful, at least in terms of delivering quality. My sampling suggests that the Starbucks supermarket line of coffees not only offers less choice than the more comprehensive line Starbucks sells in its own stores, but less character and distinction as well.

Those who find it inconvenient to shop for coffee may find ordering bulk coffee by Internet or telephone useful. Consult Sources. Coffees should be ordered through the mails *only* in whole-bean form. Unprotected ground coffees are likely to be half stale by the time they land on the porch. This means that you need a good grinder to enjoy mail-order coffee; consult Chapter 7 for details on espresso grinding and grinders.

SPECIALTY STORE DECISIONS

The range of coffees offered by specialty coffee stores and Internet sites can be daunting. The reader may want to skim through the Espresso Break on Coffee Speak on pages 89–92 for an orientation to specialty coffee terminology.

For selecting among caffeine-free coffees by decaffeination method, see pages 76–78; for buying coffees that respond to various environmental or social issues see pages 72–74.

But once such concerns have been responded to, the subtler and perhaps more interesting decisions remain; what style of roast to buy; whether to buy a blended or unblended coffee; which blended or unblended coffee to buy; and finally, whether and how to assemble blends of your own.

Choosing a Roast Style

As indicated earlier, any style of roast can be prepared in an espresso machine and used to assemble espresso drinks, but only a medium-dark to dark-brown roast, darker than the typical North American roast but not black-brown, will produce the flavor we associate with espresso. See Chapter 4 for more on the process and philosophy of roasting. Coffees roasted toward the lighter end of the espresso spectrum retain some of the brisk, acidy tones characteristic of medium-roasted coffees; coffees roasted near the middle of the spectrum lose almost all acidy notes, replacing them with the pungent yet sweet flavor complex typical of darker-roast coffees; the very darkest roasts begin to lose body and display the monotoned, charred flavor typical of these nearly black styles.

The Complex Relationship of Roast and Coffee

Choosing espresso coffee by roast is complicated by the fact that most coffees intended for the espresso cuisine are blends, and the composition of the blend may either offset or reinforce taste tendencies created by style of roast. Generally, those roasters who prefer a mild, sweet espresso will pursue their objective on two fronts. They will use coffees with low acidity in their blends, and will also bring that blend of low-acidity coffees to a relatively light espresso roast to avoid provoking the bitter notes characteristic of darker roasts. On the other hand, those who prefer sharpness and punch in their espresso blends may use highly acidy coffees *and* bring those acidy blends to a relatively dark roast, thus emphasizing both acidity and the bitter side of the bittersweet dark-roast flavor equation. The effect of roast on coffee flavor can only be fully understood by roasting coffee oneself, or by finding a roaster who offers the same straight or unblended coffees in a variety of styles of roast.

BLENDED VS. UNBLENDED COFFEES IN ESPRESSO

Most of those who qualify as espresso experts argue for the superiority of blended espresso coffees over unblended. Their arguments often appear self-serving, however, since most experts are also in the business of selling coffee, and blends have several advantages for the coffee seller. First, they enable the seller to develop a loyalty to a certain blend, rather than loyalty to a more generic unblended single-origin coffee; second, they promote a mystification of the blending and roasting process, both of which are somewhat simpler than roasters make them out to be; and three, blends enable the more cost-conscious roaster to cut costs while maintaining quality.

Given all of that, good blends doubtless do pro-duce a more satisfying espresso over the long haul, at least for those who prefer consistency over experiment and surprise. But for those who enjoy variety, unblended dark-roasted coffees themselves, plus the opportunity they afford for creating one's own blends, offer an exciting opportunity for connoisseurship.

Espresso blends and blending are discussed in detail on pages 70–72. Once the issues and principles of espresso blending are understood, the next step is actually tasting a variety of blends. Espresso blends vary dramatically from roaster to roaster.

SINGLE-ORIGIN COFFEES IN ESPRESSO

Unblended, single-origin coffees consist of beans from one crop and one origin in one country. Most specialty stores carry a small selection of such unblended coffees brought to a dark roast suitable for espresso. They are usually identified by double- and triple-decker names like *Dark-Roast Sumatra Mandheling, French-Roast Colombian Supremo,* or *Organic Guatemala Antigua Dark.*

With some roasters, most notably the influential West Coast Peet's Coffee chain, *all* coffees in the store are roasted dark, and consequently all can yield an interesting espresso. At this writing many roasters are imitating Peet's extreme dark-roast style. Unfortunately, most of these dark-roasters-come-lately do not understand the style as well as the Peet's roasters do, are too aggressive with the roast, and end up burning the beans. These dry, brittle beans produce a thin-bodied, bitter espresso. If you find a store in which all of the coffees are roasted dark-brown-bordering-on-black, try a half-pound as espresso, but don't be surprised if the results are unsatisfactory and you need to go elsewhere for a coffee that produces a full, round, sweet beverage.

With coffee companies that don't roast everything dark, the key terms identifying darker styles of roast appropriate for espresso are either obvious color words like *dark* or *dark-roast;* European geography names like *Viennese, Italian, French;* or (most explicitly) *espresso.* Any coffee preceded by these adjectives will make a plausible espresso, although those that are extremely dark, almost black, may produce a thin-bodied, bitter cup. For a summary of names for roast see the table on page 57. For more on coffee names generally see pages 89–92.

Around the World in a Demitasse

For those interested in exploring single-origin coffees as espressos, here is an overview of the better-known coffees of the world from an espresso perspective.

Powerfully Acidy Coffees. The best-known are Kenyas, Strictly Hard Bean Costa Ricas and Guatemalas, Yemen mochas, and the better Colombias. These are all high-grown, dense-bean coffees that display bright, acidy notes in nut-brown roasts and turn intensely bittersweet in dark-brown styles. They may be a bit overwhelming as a straight espresso but will carry through almost any amount of milk and make excellent highlight coffees in espresso blends. Unlike Kenya and the Latin America coffees, Yemen coffees are dry-processed or dried inside the fruit, which may

account for the way they often round out a darker roast better than many Kenyas or high-grown Central Americas. Straight Yemen brought to a moderately dark roast can make a superb espresso.

Classic Coffees with Gentler Profiles Most Caribbean coffees (Puerto Rico, Jamaica Blue Mountain, Dominican, Haiti, etc.), Mexicos, El Salvadors, Nicaraguas, Panamas, Perus, are wet-processed coffees with a bright but gentle acidity usually easily tamed by dark-roasting. The sweeter versions of these coffees will make a pleasant espresso, relatively light-bodied but round and lively. Some Perus produce a particularly agreeable demitasse.

Brazil Coffees. The finest Brazil coffees—low-acid, sweet, round, full-bodied—are espresso treasures. These coffees, which come into their own only when roasted and brewed as espresso, are grown on a handful of medium-to-large Brazilian farms, come from trees of the traditional Bourbon variety, and are dry- or "natural"-processed. They must be roasted tactfully to preserve their sweetness and will not tolerate extremely dark roast styles. But if everything is right these dry-processed Brazil Bourbons are among the most exquisite of espresso-inclined origins.

Hawaii Coffees. America's obsession with its home-grown coffee leads me to give it its own category. Hawaii Kona, one of the world's most expensive coffees, is hardly ever presented as espresso because its high-priced subtleties are lost in a darker roast. However, you will find Konas dark-roasted simply because the people who roast them don't know any better. If you do try one of these inadvertently dark-roasted Konas as espresso, and if it hasn't been destroyed in the roasting, it will yield a pleasant if light-bodied demitasse. On the other hand, some of the very best Konas are rather acidy coffees that make a powerful, bittersweet espresso along high-grown Costa Rica lines. Coffees from large farms outside the Kona district, on the islands of Kauai, Molokai, and Maui, are less expensive, available directly from the growers in dark-roast styles, and can make interesting espressos if the roast is handled carefully.

Indonesia and India Coffees. Coffees from the gigantic Indonesian islands of Sumatra and Sulawesi (old name Celebes) can make splendid espresso: full-bodied, sweet yet pungent, complex. The problem is finding *good* Sumatras and Sulawesis. Along with the rich, complex, sweet versions, many cheap, harsh-tasting Sumatras and Sulawesis find their way into North America. But there is no doubt that the best and sweetest rank with the finest dry-processed Brazils as the most desirable of espresso origins.

Wet-processed coffees from Java and Papua New Guinea produce sweet but lighter-bodied espressos than the best Sumatras and Sulawesis. India coffees are typically low-toned and display sweetness and body but may come off as a bit inert.

Ethopias and other African Coffees. Kenya coffees are in a class of their own: powerfully acidy, deeply resonant, alive with wine and (on occasion) berry notes, and wonderfully consistent. Typically, however, they are too acidy or (in a dark roast) too pungent for espresso brewing on their own. Ethiopia coffees tend to be fragrant, relatively light-bodied, and can make very interesting and elegantly nuanced espresso. The famous and distinctive Ethiopia Yirgacheffe, with its extraordinary floral perfumes, may be a touch too light-bodied for espresso, but can add wonderfully tantalizing high notes to a blend. Other African coffees, like Zimbabwes and Malawis, are wine- or fruit-toned coffees that make interesting but also relatively light-bodied espressos.

Robustas. The best coffees from the *Coffea canephora* or Robusta species imported into the United States are grown in the Ivory Coast, Thailand, and India. You will not find them for sale as single-origin coffees, however. If you are a home roaster and you manage to turn some up as green coffee and roast them, you will discover that they are heavy, flat, and inert. Some professional blenders condemn them. Others claim that they add resonance to an espresso blend, forming an unheard but amplifying sounding board for more assertive notes.

Aged and Monsooned Coffees. These specially handled coffees (see page 69) are usually too heavy and monotoned on their own, but in small quantities can add weight and complexity to blends.

A BLEND OF YOUR OWN

Having sampled some dark-roasted blends and unblended single-origins, readers may be interested in

The open counter of the old Peerless Coffee Company in Oakland, California, an excellent example of the small storefront coffee-roasting establishments that were a familiar feature of North American shopping districts during the nineteenth and early twentieth centuries. A few, like Peerless, survived to join the current revival of specialty coffee roasting. Peerless Coffee, still family-owned, now occupies a large plant a few blocks from its original home.

experimenting with their own blends. Most specialty stores will be happy to combine coffees for customers, providing the requests don't become too complicated.

To create your own espresso blend, you might start with a base of dark-roast Brazil bourbons (dry-processed, often marketed as Brazil Bourbon Santos), Mexico, or Peru, then experiment by asking the clerk to add varying proportions of other beans. Twenty percent of an acidy, winy Africa coffee like Kenya plus perhaps another 20 percent of a pungently low-toned coffee like Sumatra or Sulawesi, both in either a dark or a medium-dark "full city" roast, combined with 60 percent dark-roast Brazil, Mexico, or Peru, make an interesting and lively blend. Experiment with the proportions of Sumatra and Kenya until you obtain a balance that satisfies you. Or try 10 percent Kenya and 20 percent Ethiopia Yirgacheffe, to add floral notes at the top of the profile as well as fruity mid-tones. For more ideas, look over the preceding section on Single-Origin Coffees in Espresso.

Those who are not all-out purists may enjoy adding small proportions of flavored beans to a personal espresso blend. Ten percent chocolate or hazelnut-flavored beans, for example, contribute an interesting flavor note, although the aftertaste may be cloying to an experienced palate.

ESPRESSO BREAK
COFFEE SPEAK: THE SPECIALTY COFFEE LEXICON

Variety, one of the attractions of specialty coffee, can also be one of its frustrations. Most specialty stores carry at least twenty different coffees; some may carry as many as fifty. The best Internet sites carry even more. The sheer babble of names and (in the case of the stores) the repetitive shades of brown in the bins can intimidate and confuse. Here are a few rules of thumb to assist in making sense of specialty coffee cacophony.

European Names. These usually describe blends of dark-roast coffee. *Viennese, Italian, French, Neapolitan, Spanish,* and *European* are all frequently used names for generic blends of coffee roasted darker than the (usually unnamed) American roast. *Espresso* and *Continental* are also popular names for generic dark roast blends. Most coffees described by these terms are suitable for espresso cuisine; choosing from among them is a matter of taste. See the Espresso Break on pages 56–57 for a complete list of roast names, and Chapter 4 for more on roasting and styles of roast.

Non-European Names. These usually describe unblended or single-origin coffees. Coffees sold in straight or unblended form, also called *single-origin* or varietal coffees, typically carry the name of the country in which they were grown: *Kenya, Colombia, Costa Rica,* etc. If these coffees have been brought to a darker roast suitable for the espresso cuisine, they usually carry a double-decker name: *Dark-Roast Kenya, Colombia Dark Roast,* etc. For some advice on choosing among unblended dark-roast coffees see Chapter 6.

Most unblended or single origin coffees also carry a subordinate set of names intended to narrow the growing geography a bit, and spice up the sales pitch on signs and brochures. These names usually represent market names, of which there are thousands in the coffee trade, or grade names, which are only a bit less numerous and confusing than market names, or estate names, which are the names of the farms where the coffees have been grown and processed.

Market names usually refer to the region or district in which the coffee is grown (Mexico *Coatepec*), the main market town in that region (Guatemala *Antigua*), the port through which the coffee is shipped (Brazil *Santos*), or none of the above, which means that the original geographical source of the name has been lost in the mists of time and preserved principally on the burlap of coffee sacks and in the jargon of coffee traders.

Grade names usually refer to the altitude at which the coffee is grown (particularly in central America); to the size of the bean; to numbers of defects (discolored beans, sticks, pebbles, etc.); to the nature of the processing (wet-processing vs. dry-processing); or to cup quality, or how clean and characteristic of the region the coffee tastes.

Altitude is reflected in grading terms like *high grown, hard bean* (the higher the growing altitude the denser and harder the bean), and *altura* (Spanish for "height" or "summit"). Grade names keyed to bean size usually are alphabetical (*A* is the highest grade in India: *AA* the highest in Kenya, Tanzania, and New Guinea; *AAA* in Peru). Wet-processed coffees tend to be differentiated from dry-processed coffees by relatively self-evident terms like *washed* and the Spanish term for washed, *lavado*. Finally, some grading systems may simply employ a hierarchy of superlatives (in Colombia *supremo* is the best grade, *extra* is second-best, and *excelso* a grade combining beans from both).

To summarize, names may appear like the following: *Kenya AA Dark-Roast* (a high-grade Kenyan coffee brought to a dark roast suitable for espresso cuisine); *French-Roast Oaxaca Pluma* (a wet-processed coffee from the Mexican state of Oaxaca brought to an extremely dark roast);

Espresso-Roast Sumatra Lintong (a Sumatra coffee that bears the market name Lintong and has been brought to a roast suitable for espresso); and so on.

A brief discussion of single origin coffees and their suitability for espresso brewing appears on pages 86–87. For more detail on single-origin coffees and their cup characteristics see the companion volume to this book, *Coffee: A Guide to Buying, Brewing, Enjoying*.

Fanciful, Whimsical, or Arbitrarily Romantic Names. These usually describe house blends. In an effort to establish brand loyalty and develop a company mystique most specialty roasters offer house blends, mysteriously named and usually vaguely described ("An exotic blend of robust Indonesian, pungent East African, and brisk Central American growths, carefully proportioned and roasted to bring out the full power and bouquet of these rare and exotic origins. Named after the roastmaster's favorite niece"). These blends are usually excellent and worth trying. I only wish the copy writers patronized less and communicated more. Many of these proprietary blends are dark-roast and intended for espresso cuisine.

Cocktail or Candy Names. These describe flavored coffees, decent-quality arabica coffees brought to a medium roast, then coated with various flavoring agents. The flavorings are variations of those used in countless other foods. Sometimes nut fragments are added to the flavored beans to dress them up. The names for flavored coffees (*Piña Colada,*

Vanilla Nut, Frangelica Cream) attempt to evoke associations with pleasurable experiences like vacations and dessert, and usually are as carefully contrived as the flavorings themselves. Many specialty roasters refuse to have flavored coffees in their stores; others carry them with varying degrees of enthusiasm.

Since most flavored coffees are brought to a medium roast, they do not figure prominently in espresso cuisine. Some espresso drinkers like to add small quantities of flavored beans to their espresso blends before grinding. See Chapter 9 for a general overview on the use of flavorings in espresso cuisine.

Names for Decaffeination Processes and Social and Environmental Programs. Still another layer of coffee naming has been created by decaffeination processes and organic and other ecologically progressive growing practices.

Decaffeinated or caffeine-free coffees have had the caffeine soaked out of them; they are delivered to the roaster green, like any other coffee. Roasters in most metropolitan centers offer a variety of coffees in decaffeinated form. The origin of the beans and style of roast should still be designated: *Decaf French-Roast Colombia,* for instance, or *Decaffeinated Dark-Roast Special House Blend,* etc. See pages 75–78 for details on the various decaffeination processes and their common retail names.

Properly defined, *organic coffees* are those coffees certified by various international monitoring agencies as having been grown without the use of agricultural chemicals. "Bird Friendly" is a trademark of the Smithsonian Institution that identifies organically grown coffees which also have been grown under mixed-species shade trees. Particularly in Central and South America, these trees provide shelter and forage for migrating songbirds. *Shade-grown* is a much vaguer term that means that a coffee has been, according to the seller, grown under a canopy of trees—any kind of trees—rather than in full sun. *Fair Trade Certified* coffees are certified to have been purchased from farmers at prices that, according to a formula prescribed by a consortium of international agencies, give the farmers a reasonable return for their product. *Eco-OK* coffees are certified by an arm of the Rainforest Alliance to meet an array of balanced environmental and economic criteria intended to assure the well-being of both land and people. An even broader set of criteria is in process of being defined and codified under the general term *sustainable*, although at this writing that term, like *shade-grown*, is not limited by any mechanism for definition and certification. In other words, it currently means whatever the user wants it to mean, although that laissez faire situation may change. For more on these issue coffees, see pages 72–74.

Terms like *organic* and *shade-grown* are qualifiers added to all the rest of the adjectives possible to pile onto a specialty coffee name. So, if you're ready for this, in a specialty store it might be possible to see a coffee named *Dark-Roast Swiss Water-Process Decaffeinated Shade-Grown Organic Mexico Chiapas,* describing a Mexico coffee from the state of Chiapas that has been grown under mixed shade cover and processed without the use of chemicals, has been treated to remove the caffeine by use of hot water and charcoal filtering, and has been brought to a dark roast suitable for espresso cuisine.

Because specialty coffee roasters justifiably question the viability of their customers' attention span when confronted with such breathless nomenclature, multiple qualifying terms are usually dispersed in the signage system, relegated to the fine print, or condensed by leaving something out.

Some Other Terms. Here are a last few terms that defy easy categorization: *Turkish coffee* usually refers to neither coffee from Turkey nor style of roast. The name designates grind of coffee and style of brewing. *Turkish* is a common name for a medium- to dark-roast coffee, ground to a powder, sweetened, boiled, and served with the sediment still in the cup. As indicated earlier, *Viennese* usually describes a somewhat darker than normal roast, but it can also describe a blend of roasts (about half dark and half medium), or, in Great Britain, a blend of coffee and roast fig. *New Orleans coffee* is either a dark-roast coffee mixed with roast chicory root or a dark-roast, usually Brazilian-based, blend without chicory.

7 FUSSY AS A FRENCH OMELET COOK

GRINDING COFFEE FOR ESPRESSO

When one of my coffee books was published in Great Britain, a reviewer for the *Manchester Guardian* accused me of being "as fussy as a French omelet cook" about coffee. There is obviously some cultural bias at work here (do French people accuse one another of being as fussy as an English umbrella maker?). I also think coffee is considerably more noble and important than omelets, even French omelets. Nevertheless, whenever I find myself about to launch into some detailed set of coffee prescriptions, that quote comes painfully to mind.

This is one of those moments. To those whose only coffee-making experience has been with brewing methods other than espresso, the remarks I am about to make concerning the importance of the correct grind in espresso will doubtless sound like the mutterings of a French omelet cook, even an obsessive French omelet cook. So be it, because grinding the coffee may be the single most important act in the entire sequence of espresso brewing events.

Recall that the heavy body and rich flavor of espresso coffee is achieved through pressure and resistance: pressure by the brewing water, and resistance to that pressure by a uniform layer of compressed, ground coffee. The hot water, under great pressure, does its best to push its way through the layer of ground coffee, but owing to the resistance of the finely ground and highly compressed coffee, it cannot succeed until it has saturated every grain of the coffee, extracting the coffee's entire flavor and perfume almost instantly, and delivering it intact into the cup. This perfectly poised opposition of pressure and resistance is at the heart of the espresso brewing system.

THE IDEAL GRIND

The ideal grind for espresso is: (1) a grit just short of powder; (2) a relatively uniform grit in terms of size of grain; and (3) a grit made up of flaked or shaved, rather than torn or compressed, grains.

These three criteria are listed in order of importance. Criterion 1, the proper grind overall, is crucial to any degree of success in espresso brewing. An overly coarse grind will permit the water to gush through the coffee bed and will produce a thin, bitter cup; a powdery grind will slow the brewing process to the point that only dark, burned-tasting dribbles will escape the filter holder.

However, the optimum grind varies somewhat according to the nature of the brewing apparatus. Larger, more expensive pump and piston machines (categories 3 and 4, pages 107–12) require a finer grind than the relatively inexpensive, steam-pressure apparatus (categories 1 and 2, pages 106–7). The larger machines generate 9 or more atmospheres of pressure, whereas the steam-pressure devices only muster about 1½ to perhaps 3 atmospheres. The greater the pressure, the finer and more compacted the coffee bed must be to take full advantage of the pressure-resistance equilibrium of the espresso method.

Criterion 2, uniform grind, also varies in importance depending on the sophistication of the brewing equipment. The greater the pressure exerted by the machine, the more uniform the grind needs to be. Small steam-pressure machines will make a reasonably flavorful espresso with a relatively inconsistent grind of the kind produced by inexpensive home grinders. The larger pump and piston machines require a much more uniform grind, which can be produced only by a commercial grinder or by one of the more expensive specialized home espresso grinders.

Criterion 3, flaked grains versus torn or crushed grains, may be a typically French-omelet-cook point, yet it remains an important point. There is no doubt that a grind that is produced by shaving the bean into relatively uniform flakes is superior to a grind produced by crushing the bean or tearing it into irregular pieces. The flaked configuration absorbs water more quickly and completely than the more rounded, compressed grains produced by crushed beans, and more consistently than the irregular grains produced by tearing the beans. Flaked grains are produced by burr grinders with sharp, high-quality burrs. Torn grains are produced by inexpensive blade grinders, and crushed or compressed grains either by good burr grinders with dull burrs, or by cheap burr grinders whose burrs were dull to start with.

It is true that a grind that is correct and uniform, albeit compressed rather than shaved, will produce decent quality espresso, but the finest beverage will only be produced by a properly flaked grind.

GRINDING OPTIONS

Ground espresso coffee can be obtained in one of four ways: (1) by buying whole-bean coffees and grinding them at home just before brewing; (2) by buying whole-bean coffees and having them ground on a large-scale commercial machine; (3) by buying pre-ground, canned coffees; (4) by buying espresso "pods," little serving-sized paper bags of pre-ground coffee designed to fit in specially designed filters supplied with some home pump machines.

There is no doubt that buying fresh whole-bean coffees, storing them correctly, and grinding them just before brewing produces the freshest and most flavorful coffee of any kind, including espresso. The problem with applying this formula to espresso brewing is the precision required of the grind.

The little electric blade grinders so common now in North American homes, used with care, will produce a grind sufficiently fine and uniform to produce decent, albeit thin-bodied, espresso on simple brewing devices that work by steam pressure only (categories 1 and 2, pages 106–7). However, larger pump or piston machines (categories 3 and 4, pages 107–12) require a much more precise grind to operate to their full potential. Buyers of pump or piston brewers should purchase one of the more expensive classes of grinders described below under the heading "Home Grinder for Pump and Piston Machines."

Whole-bean coffees custom ground in a large, commercial grinder at the point of purchase are the next best alternative to grinding at home. Specialty coffee stores are preferable to supermarkets as a source for such coffees, since specialty stores usually maintain their grinding apparatus better than do supermarkets, and stock fresher beans.

However, if you do buy at a supermarket or fancy food store and set the grinder yourself, make certain to turn it to the setting indicated for "espresso." If there is no espresso setting indicated, turn to the finest setting and touch the grinder on for a second or two, catching a bit of the ground coffee. It should be a grit but not a powder. If you obtain a powder, back off one notch before grinding the rest of your coffee. Some commercial grinders offer two adjustments for espresso, a finer and a coarser. Set the grinder to the finer of the two adjustments if you have a pump or piston machine, the coarser if you are using a simpler machine that forces the water through the coffee with steam pressure.

Canned espresso coffees are a reasonable third alternative if purchased carefully. Some canned coffees are totally inadequate for espresso brewing because they are ground too coarsely. Read the fine print on the can before you buy. If the label says something like "suitable for all brewing methods," return the can to the shelf forthwith. Cans that read "extra-fine grind for espresso brewers," or words to that effect, may contain something worth packing in a filter.

Owners of some pump machines also have the option of using espresso pods, one-serving paper sacks filled with pre-ground coffee. From the point of view of freshness, pods are the least attractive option, since the coffee usually has been roasted and ground in faraway places and held for long periods in foil envelopes. Espresso brewed from such pods definitely will not display the explosive perfume of espresso brewed from freshly ground, whole-bean coffee. Pods also represent the most costly way to brew espresso. On the other hand, they do eliminate a good deal of fussing, and may be a good temporary approach for beginners. If you buy pods, make certain they are either specifically designed for the pump machine you

own, or, if your machine specifies that it uses pods following the ESE (Easy Serving Espresso) standard, make sure you buy ESE-compatible pods.

HOME GRINDERS

The demands of espresso brewing create a great divide among coffee grinders. On one side are those capable of producing a grind sufficiently fine and uniform for steam pressure brewers only (categories 1 and 2, pages 106–7). On the other are those capable of consistently producing the more precise grind demanded by higher pressure pump and piston machines (categories 3 and 4, pages 107–12). *If you buy or own an espresso brewer, make sure you buy a grinder with equivalent capability.*

Electric Blade Grinders

As I write, these inexpensive, versatile household tools sell for $10 to $25. Rather than grinding the coffee between burrs, they whack the coffee to pieces with blades that rotate at a very high speed, like blender blades. These devices can also be used to pulverize spices and softer nuts.

Electric blade grinders, *used knowledgeably,* will produce a grind appropriate for the steam-pressure brewers in categories 1 and 2, pages 106–7. They cannot be used with higher pressure pump and piston machines.

When using these devices, grind the coffee in relatively brief bursts. It also helps to gently bounce the bottom of the grinder on the counter between bursts to knock the coffee that often cakes up around the

Electric blade grinder

blades or at the edges of the receptacle back down to where the blades can reach it. When you first use a blade grinder for espresso, you will need to regularly check the fineness of the grind. It is usually impossible to visually confirm the correct gritty grind without taking the top off the grinder, even with models that provide a sort of magnifying glass lid. You periodically must pull a pinch out of the receptacle and rub it or look at it. Again, it should be a fine grit, just short of powder. You can never obtain a perfectly consistent grind with these devices, by the way, so don't waste time trying. When the average particle is grit, and the rest is either in powder or larger pieces, carry on with the brewing.

The effort required in getting the ground coffee out from under the blades of these devices also can be trying. However, I find little evidence for another accusation leveled at blade grinder: Some claim that they heat the coffee as they pulverize it, destroying valuable aromatic oils. It is difficult to believe that the (at most) mild warmth these devices impart to coffee while reducing it to a fine grind could have a negative effect on flavor.

General Purpose Electric Burr Grinders

These devices are designed to grind coffee for a variety of brewing methods, and at this writing retail for $35 to $100. Rather than whacking the coffee to pieces, they feed the beans between motor-driven, conical burrs; the ground coffee sprays out into the receptacle at the base of the unit.

Although these machines produce a much more uniform and consistent grind than blade grinders, most will not produce a grind sufficiently fine for pump and piston machines, and are only appropriate for use with steam-pressure brewers (categories 1 and 2, pages 106–7). At this writing one general purpose burr grinder does produce a grind sufficiently fine and uniform for all types of espresso brewers, including pump and piston: The Bunn Deluxe BCG. However, the Bunn BCG costs almost as much as a specialized espresso grinder and has vaguely marked, difficult-to-see grind settings.

Other excellent general purpose burr grinders available at this writing, like the Pavoni PA and the Capresso, only will frustrate users of pump and piston machines with their almost-fine-enough but not-quite performance. I strongly recommend that those who own or intend to purchase a pump or piston machine buy a grinder specifically designed for espresso brewing.

Hand Box Grinders

Box grinders are literally wooden boxes with cranks protruding from the top. As you turn the crank, the beans work their way down between two metal cone-shaped burrs, one rotating inside the other. The ground coffee falls into a little drawer at the bottom of the box. Some heavier versions have external metal housings and a flywheel crank on the side, like old-time store grinders.

The best and most expensive ($50 and up) of these devices make a consistent, properly flaked espresso grind appropriate for the low-pressure brewers in categories 1 and 2, pages 106–7]. The Zassenhaus line will produce an acceptable grind even for pump and piston machines if you are patient and don't mind cranking for a couple of minutes straight. At the finest setting the beans tend to feed very slowly, which prolongs the grinding process. Still, for those who argue (logically) that the best way to exercise is to do something useful like mow the lawn by hand rather than jog or jump rope, the Zassenhaus grinders might make a reasonable choice for any kind of espresso brewing, including pump and piston. The design that you can hold between the knees while cranking is easiest to use.

High-End Burr Grinders Designed for Espresso Brewing

If you are pursuing a true caffè-quality espresso, you will need to pony up the $120 to $300 required

General-purpose electric burr grinder

Manual box grinder

Electric burr grinder, specially designed for espresso brewing. The cylinder at the front of the device is a doser, or ground coffee dispenser.

erly, and are adjustable in fine enough increments so that aficionados can fine-tune their grind setting to accommodate changes in ambient humidity and moisture content in the beans.

The majority of these grinders also include a spring-loaded doser, a device that dispenses a serving's worth (a dose) of ground coffee with a flick of a lever. Some also include an attached tamper to distribute and press the coffee into the filter.

Both of these features are useful, provided they match the filter holder and filter of the machine you own or intend to purchase. Dosers have a cradlelike device that holds the filter holder in position to receive the dose of ground coffee. Make sure that you try the filter holder from the machine you own or intend to own to make certain that it fits the doser cradle of the grinder you are considering buying. Surprising mismatches occur, even between grinders and machines from the same manufacturer.

As for the tamper, its overall diameter should more or less match the diameter of the filter from your machine. If not, continue to use the tamper that the manufacturer of your machine provided.

A specialized espresso grinder may be a useful purchase even if the doser offers the wrong fit for your machine's filter holder, since most of the grinders in this class provide the option of replacing the doser with an (included) lidded receptacle, from which you simply spoon the coffee into the filter.

for a proper, heavy-duty espresso grinder. The Saeco 2002 is as good as any, and one of the least expensive in its class. These devices are appropriate for all categories of espresso brewer. They flake the coffee prop-

ESPRESSO BREAK

KEEPING IT FRESH

Every step of the transformation of green coffee into hot brewed coffee makes the flavor essence of the bean more vulnerable to destruction. Green coffees keep for years, with only a slow, subtle change in flavor. But roasted coffee begins to lose flavor after a week, ground coffee an hour after grinding, and brewed coffee in minutes, even seconds.

One of the many technical superiorities of the espresso system is its emphasis on freshness: each cup is not only brewed on demand, but the coffee for each cup is *ground* on demand as well. In the finest of traditional Italian caffès, the coffee was also roasted on the premises, pushing the emphasis on freshness to its logical conclusion. For those who are sufficiently enthusiastic and patient to roast their own espresso coffee at home, see pages 53–56 for a brief introduction to that practice.

THE FREEZER CONTROVERSY

Most of us buy our coffee already roasted, however, either in whole-bean form or pre-ground. The question of how to maintain freshness in this fragile substance has produced one of the more vigorous and amusing of pop food debates, with advocates of the "airtight container in a cool dry place" position doing battle with "keep it in the freezer" advocates, and both attacking the cavalier thoughtlessness of those who simply chuck their coffee into the refrigerator next to the milk and carrots.

The refrigerator position is the easiest to demolish. Moisture is the enemy of roasted coffee. The flavor "oils" in roasted coffee are very delicate, volatile water-soluble substances that moisture immediately dilutes and odors taint. Refrigerators tend to be both damp and odorous. Those who automatically toss everything perishable into the refrigerator upon liberating it from the grocery sack definitely should modify that reflex in regard to coffee.

The airtight container in a cool dry place makes most sense in the case of coffee that has already been ground, or whole-bean coffee used on a day-by-day basis. On the other hand, the freezer makes sense for whole-bean coffee that you do not intend to consume immediately.

Some Informal Experiments

In my admittedly informal experiments, whole-bean coffees placed in a freezer in a sealed bag immediately after roasting seem to last virtually without flavor loss for about a month, then begin a slow deterioration. In a few months the flavor loss is clear and dramatic. My tests were run using a first-rate freezer, however. Small refrigerator freezers are subject to frequent temperature changes as the door opens and closes, and may not produce such consistent results.

At any rate, dodging the tomatoes tossed by my opponents in this important debate (all the more dangerous because they are doubtless *frozen* tomatoes), I advise readers to buy small lots of freshly roasted coffee and keep that coffee in sealed containers (*genuinely* sealed containers, the kind with rubber gaskets and clamp-down lids) in a cool dry place, out of direct sunlight. If, however, you shop for coffee less frequently than the righteous coffee lover truly ought to, and if you keep your whole-bean coffee around for more than a week before you consume it, place it in carefully sealed freezer bags in the deepest recesses of a good freezer as soon as you get it home. When you are ready to brew, separate only as many beans as you plan to use immediately and allow them to thaw before grinding them. Put the rest back in the freezer.

8 ESPRESSO AT HOME

BREWING APPARATUS

ooner or later those who enjoy espresso at caffès and bars begin to think about making their own espresso drinks at home. For many the prospect may appear intimidating. The caffè machines hiss, produce alarming noises, and are large, complex, and obviously expensive.

Home espresso brewing, although more complex than many culinary procedures, is not difficult in the long run. It does require some patience, however, both in the selection of gear and in mastering various procedures. And, as with most undertakings dependent on technology, the more you spend on equipment, the less detail you need to master. Nevertheless, even those prepared to spend large sums of money on the best equipment need to master some procedure, plus understand the principles behind that procedure. Espresso is still an undertaking in which excellence needs to be learned, rather than simply bought.

This chapter and the related Espresso Break on brewing equipment (pages 113–19) offer an orientation to various classes of home espresso brewing equipment and some advice on choosing that equipment. If you already own a satisfactory espresso apparatus, skip to Chapter 9 and related Espresso Breaks for some advice and encouragement on using that apparatus.

DECIDING WHAT YOU WANT

The first step in buying an espresso brewing system is deciding what you like about espresso, and how much you are willing to spend to get it at home.

For example, if you simply like the bittersweet tang of dark-roasted coffee, and can do without the rich, heavy body of espresso-style coffee, you can get by very cheaply. All you need do is buy some dark-roasted coffee and make it in your drip brewer as you would with any other coffee. And, if you want to top it with frothed milk, you can buy a little $20 device that permits you to froth milk by pumping a plunger through it for twenty or thirty seconds (see pages 112–13).

If you do like espresso, but only mixed with lots of hot, frothed milk, you do need specialized equipment, but by espresso standards it can be relatively inexpensive. The under-$100 brewing devices in category 2, pages 106–7, used with the $20 blade grinder, and *used knowledgeably,* will produce satisfying milk-heavy drinks like caffè lattes. Such relatively inexpensive brewers will not produce a satisfying demitasse of straight espresso, however. For straight espresso and espresso-heavy drinks you need something resembling the larger household machines described in categories 3 and 4 on pages 107–12. You also need precision-ground coffee, produced either by a specialized home espresso grinder (see Chapter 7) or in the form of little one-serving bags called pods (see pages 81–82).

For those who are deeply attracted to the romance and mystique of espresso, or who entertain often and on a large scale, or who are contemplating outfitting a small office with espresso capability, a complete high-end system is a necessity, including specialized grinder with doser and a heavy-duty, refillable pump machine with cup warmer (high end of category 3, pages 108–10). A fully automatic machine (also high end of category 3) is another attractive possibility for those outfitting small offices or who entertain heavily.

Once you have an idea of what your goal is, you might familiarize yourself with the various categories of brewing equipment described on pages 30–34, then return to this chapter to glance over the discussion that follows on various points of comparison among competing designs within each category.

POINTS OF COMPARISON FOR CATEGORY 1 BREWERS

These little devices, described and illustrated on pages 113–14, produce a rather thin-bodied beverage closer to strong drip or French-press coffee than to true espresso. Nor do they offer milk-frothing capacity.

"Moka"-Style Category 1 Designs. The clearest point of comparison among the hourglass-shaped "Moka"-style pots illustrated on page 114 is the material used in the top part of the pot, which receives the freshly brewed coffee as it sputters up through the filter. The best of these designs use ceramic or glass for this part of the pot; the next best use stainless steel; the worst use aluminum. Aluminum, and to a lesser degree stainless steel, become so hot that the metal burns the first dribbles of brewed coffee, often spoiling the taste of the entire batch. Some versions of this design make the ceramic, coffee-receiving, top part of the device removable, so that it can be lifted off the rest of the pot and taken to the table.

The other point of comparison among the Moka-style pots is appearance. The international design community has been loosed on these devices. Designer versions of the Moka-style pot can cost up to $200, and are among the most visually elegant of coffee-making apparatus. Keep in mind, however, that regardless of looks and price, all of the Moka-style pots work the same way.

Other Category 1 Designs. Designs like the little pot illustrated on page 114 that deliver the coffee directly into the cup are a good idea. The cup is automatically prewarmed and the coffee is not burned by contact with hot metal. The style of pot illustrated at the bottom on page 114 has two additional advantages: First, the filter receptacle that holds the ground coffee is set off to the side of the water reservoir, which means more heat can be applied to the water without baking the ground coffee; second, the caffè-style filter holder that contains the ground coffee can be removed without disassembling the pot, which makes it easier to recharge the device with ground coffee when brewing multiple servings. Used knowledgeably, devices like this one can make excellent espresso.

POINTS OF COMPARISON FOR CATEGORY 2 MACHINES

These are small countertop steam-pressure brewers with a valve and wand for frothing milk. See page 114 for an illustrated description. Heat is provided by a built-in electric element and the coffee is held in a removable, caffè-style filter holder that clamps into the front of the brewer. The main points of comparison among these popular, widely distributed devices:

Coffee control. The best of these devices incorporate a switch or other means to cut off the flow of coffee. I would not purchase a brewer without this function, which is essential, both as a means for timing the brewing operation to prevent overextracted coffee, and as a way of diverting all of the accumulated pressure in the boiler to the milk-frothing operation once the brewing procedure is finished.

Steam control. The best of these devices have an adjustable, screw-type steam valve, which permits you to modulate the strength of the steam flow for fine-tuned control of the milk-frothing and heating operation. Some designs control the steam function with a simple on-off switch.

Special milk-frothing nozzles. Some designs seek to assist the novice milk-frother by adding various special nozzles to the end of the steam wand. All of these gadgets are essentially aerating devices that introduce room-temperature air into the coffee along with the steam. The radical designs that literally suck cold milk out of a carton and spew it out frothed into a cup are only available with some category 3 pump machines. The simpler aerating nozzles available on the machines in this category are a mixed blessing. Although they assist in the milk-frothing operation, they complicate clean-up. See the Espresso Break on milk-frothing, pages 147–52.

POINTS OF COMPARISON FOR CATEGORY 3 MACHINES

These devices, illustrated and described on pages 115–17, are genuine espresso "machines." Used properly they will produce an authentic tazzina of espresso: rich, sweet, almost syrupy in weight, and topped with a dense-textured head of golden crema. They all use a pump to drive the brewing water through the tightly packed coffee; they all provide milk-frothing apparatus; they all use a detachable, caffè-style filter and filter holder, except for those machines that are entirely (or almost entirely) automatic and do everything at the touch of a button, including grinding, loading, and tamping the coffee.

The many machines in this category offer a very wide range of features, comparison points, and prices. They can be loosely divided into three subcategories: lighter-weight, smaller machines that at this writing sell for under $200; heavier, larger machines that sell for about $250 to $500; and completely automatic machines that retail for $650 to $1,000. I will add a few words at the end of this section on fully or almost fully automatic machines. The points of comparison outlined below apply to distinctions among the many conventional, semi-automatic pump machines.

Category 3: General Points of Comparison

Materials and weight together constitute one of the main points that distinguish higher- from lower-priced designs in category 3 machines. Weight is not simply a psychological factor; the heavier the machine the less likely it is to slide away when you clamp the filter holder into the group. Italians call such lightweight machines *macchine ballante,* "dancing machines."

In the higher-priced machines the boiler is usually constructed of brass (unless the heating is accomplished by a coil in what usually is called a *thermal block* unit); in the lower-priced machines the boiler is usually made of aluminum. In the higher-priced machines the group and filter holder are heavy, and fit together authoritatively; in less expensive machines both may be a bit on the flimsy, dancing side. In the finest machines the housing is made of metal; in lower-to-medium-priced machines, it is constructed of varying weights of plastic.

I strongly recommend that you commit an extra hundred dollars or so to buying at the sturdy, heavy end of the price–quality continuum. Some of the under $200 machines I have tested have proved to be very short-lived.

The complexity and convenience of the transition between brewing and frothing functions also may be a point of comparison for pump machines. Some require the operator to hold down a button for up to thirty seconds; others require only pressing a switch, and accomplish the transition in half that time.

The water reservoir is removable in most machines, which simplifies refilling. A few of the smaller machines may have built-in reservoirs, a minor inconvenience.

Most machines provide a means for keeping the filter inside the filter holder when you knock out the spent grounds in preparation for charging the filter with another dose of ground coffee. This is a small but important feature. A few machines may not have it at all; others may incorporate a little thumb flap that needs to be held down manually as you knock out the coffee. The best filter catches utilize magnets, spring clips, or sliding tabs. The filter remains securely in place while you are brewing, but pops out easily for cleaning or for switching to another filter with larger or smaller capacity.

External design aspects vary. Some machines have a deep, removable drip tray, which accommodates a good deal of waste liquid and can be lifted out of the machine for dumping and cleaning. Other machines have a smallish drip tray that requires either unplugging the machine and carrying it to the sink or sopping up the waste liquid with repeated passes of a sponge. The steam wand of some machines is awkwardly placed, with the nozzle too close to counter or drip tray to permit easy access for a milk-frothing pitcher. This design failure can be particularly irritating for North Americans who take their espresso with large quantities of milk, and who may find themselves indulging in odd kitchen acrobatics to extract full milk pitchers out from under strangely positioned steam wands.

Category 3: Special Features

A rather bewildering variety of special features also distinguishes category 3 machines, although many constitute minor enhancements or conveniences rather than major points of comparison.

Milk-Frothing Enhancements. Various devices that fit on the steam wand to make frothing easier are described on page 115–16. A few machines come equipped with a little plastic can-shaped turbine device that sucks cold milk out of a carton or container, froths and heats it, and spews the hot froth into a pitcher or cup. These devices produce a very nicely textured, dense froth, but need to be taken apart and cleaned obsessively to prevent build-up of milk residues and are rather delicate, misfunctioning easily. In short, they are reassuring in concept, but annoying in practice. With some home machines, the Faema line for example, the little automatic frother (Faema calls it "Cappuccino Magic") can be removed and replaced with a conventional steam wand, which makes sense. However, I would strongly recommend against buying a machine that only gives you the option of an automatic frother.

Crema-Enhancing Options. Some machines also provide special filter holders that improve production of crema, the pale gold froth that covers the surface of a well-made tazzina of straight espresso. For those who prefer their espresso straight, without frothed milk, these crema-enhancing devices may be an important feature. All of the category 3 machines, used properly with fresh, precision-ground coffee, will produce some crema, but these special filter holders ensure success. For more on the crema issue, see the Espresso Break on pages 113–19.

Grind-Compensating Filter Holder. At least one currently available line of machines, the Starbucks Barista series, incorporates a filter holder that permits the user to compensate for a less-than-precise grind by moving the handle of the filter holder to the right or left, slowing down or speeding up the flow of coffee through the grounds. This is a useful feature.

Water Softeners. Calcium build-up from hard water can disable small home pump machines by clogging the pump and other components. A few machines incorporate built-in water-softening devices, which eliminate the need to decalcify the machine on a regular basis or brew with distilled water.

Cup Warmers. Some machines also come with cup warmers, which are useful, particularly for straight espresso drinkers. The little cups used for espresso must be prewarmed or they will cool the coffee and shrink the head of crema. Caffè latte and cappuccino drinkers have less to be concerned about in this regard, since the hot frothed milk partly compensates for the cooling impact of glass or cup.

Antidrip Mechanisms. The group and steam wand of some pump machines have an annoying tendency to leak slightly when the power is on. Some machines incorporate antidrip mechanisms intended to alleviate this minor incontinence.

Other Amenities. Finally, there are various amenities like accessory drawers, built-in tampers, and knockout drawers for spent grounds. Tampers are the little disk-shaped devices used to press the ground coffee into the filter. Tampers protruding from the side of lightweight machines are frustrating because both tamper and machine tend to jitter away when you try to put a firm tamp on a dose of coffee. I prefer hand-held tampers. Built-in knock-out drawers for spent grounds would be useful if they weren't usually too flimsy to take a good knock.

The Pod Option. In the world of espresso, *pods* are neither alien egg sacs nor spaceship components, but rather pre-packed, one-serving pouches of pre-ground espresso coffee. Some manufacturers may call their pods *capsules* or other alternative space-age names. Whatever they are called, pods eliminate the most troublesome aspect of espresso brewing, which is grinding, dosing, and tamping the coffee. Unfortunately, pods are expensive, deliver somewhat less-than-fresh coffee, and require a machine that comes with special pod-compatible filters.

Pod-capable machines roughly break into two categories: those that can be used *only* with pods, usually proprietary format pods, and those that permit you to switch between conventional brewing and pod brewing and accept standardized, generic pods. Machines that take the standardized format pods usually carry the ESE (Easy Serving Espresso) trademark.

If you are interested in the option of using pods, I strongly recommend that you buy a machine that gives you maximum flexibility. In other words, a machine that allows you to switch between conventional load-and-tamp brewing and pod brewing using the ESE standard.

Category 3: *Summary of Points of Comparison*
To conclude:

- How heavy is the machine? Does it have a brass boiler and metal housing? Does it appear to be sturdy enough to stand up to the use you intend to put it?
- Is the transitional procedure for moving between brewing coffee and frothing milk more lengthy or more cumbersome than the similar procedure in other machines?
- Is there an adequate catch to hold the filter in the filter holder when spent grounds are knocked out?
- If the machine offers a gadget approach to milk frothing, is it possible to remove the gadget and froth milk in the conventional manner? Is the steam control adjustable, or does it simply turn on? (Adjustable is better.) Is the steam wand easy to access?
- Is the drip tray shallow and fixed, or deep and removable? (Deep and removable is better.)
- If the machine is designed to use only pods, can it use standardized ESE-format pods, or only those proprietary-designed pods provided by the manufacturer of the machine?
- Do you find other features of the machine attractive?
- What sort of service arrangement does your seller offer? This question is particularly important in regard to more exotic or more expensive machines, which may require specialized servicing.

Of course, all of these features need to be weighed against cost. Many of us find it easy to tolerate a few missing features or awkward design solutions in a machine that costs a couple of hundred dollars less than its competitors, but is just as sturdy and fundamentally functional.

Category 3: *Fully Automatic Machines*

Calling these machines "fully automatic" may be misleading to a North American caffè latte drinker. What is fully automated is the grinding and brewing procedure. You still need to froth the milk and combine it with the coffee to produce drinks like caffè latte and cappuccino.

These automatic devices start with a standard pump machine and build into it a coffee-grinding unit similar to the specialized home espresso grinders described in Chapter 7, together with a mechanism that, at the touch of a button, does all of the fussy little things necessary to producing good espresso. It grinds the coffee, packs it into the filter, starts and stops the brewing, and dumps the spent grounds.

At this writing only three lines of fully automatic machines are imported into North America for home (as opposed to office or restaurant) use. A handsome Capresso model sells for around $900 and the Gaggia Automatica for $1,200. The well-established Saeco line ranges in price from $650 to $1,000. All Saeco automatic models use the same sturdy, serviceable brewing mechanism, but higher-priced models add more power, permitting you to brew coffee and froth milk at the same time rather than switching between the two functions. Higher-priced models also incorporate a second reservoir for pre-ground coffee, which allows switching between a whole-bean coffee in one reservoir and a second, pre-ground coffee (de-

caffeinated, for example) in the second. This last feature is useful when entertaining, since you can switch between regular and decaffeinated coffee at the touch of a button. Finally, higher-priced models have more sophisticated digital controls.

POINTS OF COMPARISON FOR CATEGORY 4 MACHINES

Those who choose one of these romantically old-fashioned devices (see pages 118–19 for a description and illustration) love their appearance and charming directness and value their solidity.

At this writing machines in this category retail for about $450 to $800, depending on the following points of comparison:

Boiler Capacity. Since these devices need to be cooled down before being refilled, and once refilled take ten minutes or more to achieve brewing temperature, a large capacity boiler is a distinct advantage for those who entertain.

Pressure/Temperature Control and Pressure Gauge. Most machines in this category incorporate a pressure-sensitive temperature control that adjusts heat in the boiler to maintain relatively even steam pressure in the boiler. This feature permits you to leave the machine turned on for prolonged periods, sparing you a long wait for it to heat up, and probably saving on energy costs as well. More expensive machines also incorporate a pressure gauge, a wonderfully retro, industrial revolution–style dial that give you a reading of steam pressure. This last feature is not essential, but it is both picturesque and reassuring. The more we know about steam pressure the better.

Piston Mechanism. At this writing two machines in this category, the Riviera Bristol and the Electra, offer a true spring-loaded piston mechanism, whereas others simply use the muscle power of the operator to force the brewing water through the coffee. The spring-loaded design exerts considerably more pressure on the brewing water than the muscle-only models, but demands a skillful operator and a precise grind to take advantage of that pressure. For espresso beginners I would recommend the much more forgiving manual piston designs like the widely distributed Pavoni Europiccola.

Appearance. The romantic appearance of these devices, with their pipes, valves, and levers, is one of the main reasons many people prefer them to the more reticent-looking pump machines. Manufacturers cater to this appeal by adding fancy finishes and exotic ornament to some models, including gold plate, brass eagles, etc.

STAND-ALONE MILK FROTHING DEVICES

With the popularity of caffè latte, chai, and other big-milk drinks, an array of stand-alone devices have appeared on appliance shelves that produce only frothed milk, without the espresso. You can use them to add frothed milk to your drip or French-press cof-fee, for example, producing what American coffee culture calls a *café au lait*. Or you can produce frothed milk for chai, or for moos, which are essentially flavored caffè lattes with the espresso left out.

Some milk frothers are simply stovetop steam boilers with valve and wand. You use them to heat and froth milk just as you would any of the espresso brewers in categories 2 through 4, as outlined on pages 106–12.

Other frothing devices take a very different approach. With the most popular design, you pour milk into a glass or metal decanter and pump a sort of perforated piston through it until it is frothed (about thirty seconds). These devices have no agreed-on name. Asking the clerk for a "pumping milk frother" will probably get you to the right shelf in the store.

These gadgets are reassuring to milk-frothing novices because all they ask is enough energy to pump a piston vigorously for thirty seconds. The froth produced is rather heavy and inert, however, satisfactory for a caffè latte but not for a classic cappuccino. Furthermore, heating the milk is a second, separate operation from frothing. The most convenient designs have no metal parts connected to the decanter; this permits you to place the decanter with the cold milk in a microwave. Designs with metal decanters require you to heat the milk on the stove or transfer it to a metal-free container for heating in the microwave. Some designs recommend that you heat the milk before frothing; others after.

I certainly wouldn't blame a beginner for buying one of these $15 to $40 devices, but if you brew espresso and if your espresso brewer incorporates a steam wand, you will find it easier and simpler over the long haul to learn to froth milk in a conventional way.

Additional stand-alone frothing devices are appearing on coffee-store shelves, and I am sure that still more will appear after this book has gone to print.

The latest is a mini battery-operated mixer, the Bon-Jour Caffè Froth Turbo. You simply stick the mixing head in (cold) milk and push a button, then track the developing froth upward with the mixing head. You still need to heat the frothed milk in the microwave, however.

ESPRESSO BREAK

FROM POT TO MACHINE

Home Espresso Apparatuses

Home brewing devices for espresso range from the modest little stovetop pots Italians call *caffettiere,* or "coffee pots," that retail for as little as $15, to fully automatic devices that produce espresso virtually equal to the best caffè production at the press of a button, and cost as much as $1,000. Most home espresso brewing devices fall between these extremes of price and capability. For purposes of analysis I've divided them into four broad categories.

CATEGORY 1: Simple Stovetop Brewers

- *Without valve for frothing and heating milk*
- *Without mechanism for controlling coffee output*
- *Brewing pressure supplied by natural build-up of steam pressure trapped in boiler*

Advantages. Some designs are very inexpensive; others are very attractive.

Disadvantages. Cannot produce espresso drinks using frothed milk; require great care to produce even passable espresso; can only brew multiple servings.

These little devices are not true espresso brewers. Unless used with the greatest care they produce a thin, bitter, overextracted coffee that only an Italian could love, and not for very long if there is an espresso bar around.

The most familiar profile is the hourglass design shown on the top of page 114 and called a *Moka-style* pot, after the model name for the most famous and widely distributed of the brewers using this design. The illustration provides a cutaway view of such a device. The water boils in the bottom part of the pot (A); the pressure of the trapped steam forces hot water up a tube and through the ground coffee held in a metal filter at the waist of the pot (B). The brewed coffee trickles out into the receptacle at the top of the pot (C).

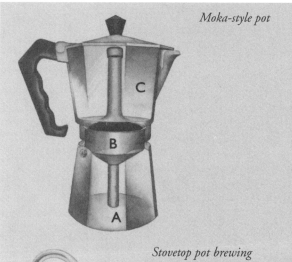

Moka-style pot

Stovetop pot brewing directly into cup

Stovetop pot incorporating caffè-style filter holder

All of the various designs illustrated here, as well as those described in later pages as category 2, work in similar fashion, using the pressure of trapped steam to force the brewing water through the coffee. All provide a brewing pressure of about 1½ to 3 atmospheres, considerably less than the 9 or more atmospheres now considered optimum for espresso brewing.

Designs like the example illustrated at the left brew the coffee directly into the cup, and designs like the devices on the bottom left brew into a separate receptacle and make use of an external, caffè-style filter holder and filter.

CATEGORY 2: Countertop Steam Pressure Brewers

- *With valve for frothing and heating milk*
- *With mechanism for controlling coffee output*
- *Brewing pressure supplied by natural build-up of steam pressure trapped in boiler*

Advantages. Relatively inexpensive; provide more predictable, stable steam pressure than stovetop models in category 1. Operated carefully can produce acceptable espresso drinks with frothed milk; can be used to froth milk or prepare hot beverages independent of the coffee-making operation.

Disadvantages. Cannot produce authentic straight espresso; require care to produce espresso acceptable for frothed milk drinks; occupy some counter space.

Devices of this design are currently the most popular of espresso brewers on the North American market. Like the category 1 stovetop devices they brew coffee using the pressure of trapped steam, but they add an electric heating element, which promotes a more consistent and safer steam pressure, and a valve and wand for frothing and heating milk. See the cross-section illustration on the bottom right. The closed boiler (A) generates steam, which forces the hot water below it out and through the ground coffee in the filter and filter holder at (B). The steam wand (C) controlled by a steam valve (D) taps the steam for milk frothing.

These brewers are designed to provide the North American "latte" and casual cappuccino drinker with an adequate drink at a reasonable price. They retail between $50 and $100. All provide a steam valve and wand for frothing and heating milk. All have an aluminum boiler or water reservoir with stainless steel filter and filter holder. All separate the filter and filter holder from the boiler to avoid overheating the ground coffee, and all have a removable, caffè-style filter and filter holder.

CATEGORY 3: Countertop Pump Machines

- *With valve for frothing and heating milk*
- *Switch-activated pump system controls coffee output*
- *Brewing pressure supplied by pump. Approximate pressure 6 to 15 atmospheres*

Advantages. Make near caffè-quality espresso and espresso drinks with frothed milk if used correctly; refillable reservoirs

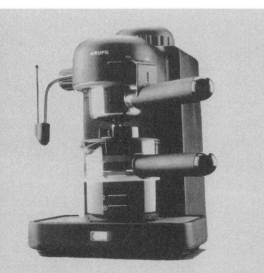

Countertop steam pressure brewer

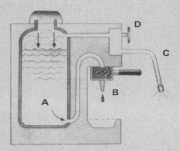

Cross-section, countertop steam pressure brewer

Typical home pump machine

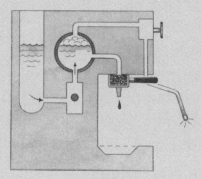

Cross-section, home pump machine

make it possible to produce any number of espresso drinks without interruption or cool-down; achieve brewing temperature relatively rapidly; brew with water held at optimum (lower-than-boiling) brewing temperature.

Disadvantages. Take up counter space; more expensive than category 2 devices; more reticent and less romantic in appearance and operation than category 4 machines; in many cases less sturdy than category 4 machines. The cheapest of these devices (under $200 at this writing) are often flimsy, and should be avoided in favor of sturdier, heavier models that (regrettably) cost a bit more.

At this point we enter the world of the true home espresso machine. All of the devices in this and the following category 4 provide means to press the hot water through the coffee bed at pressures considerably exceeding the approximately 1½ atmospheres generated by steam pressure alone. All provide steam valves and wands; all utilize separate caffè-style filters and filter holders that can be repeatedly charged with ground coffee for multiple "pulls" of one or two servings of espresso each.

The designs in this category provide additional pressure on the hot water by means of an electric pump; a separate function provides steam for milk-frothing. The separation of brewing and frothing functions permits the brewing water to be delivered to the coffee at the 186–192°F authorities agree is optimum for espresso brewing. Machines in other categories do not control the temperature of the brewing water as precisely as machines in this category.

In almost all pump machines the operator is asked to first brew the coffee, then activate a switch or hold down a button, which raises the heat in the boiler or heating coil from the lower brewing temperature to a higher temperature appropriate for steam production.

Internal Elements. The principal concealed elements of pump machines are indicated in the simplified diagram on the previous page: a water reservoir (A), in which the water is held at room temperature and which can be refilled while the machine is in use; a pump (B) for transferring water from reservoir to boiler and for pressing the brewing water through the coffee; a small boiler (C) for heating water for brewing and steam production; and various control mechanisms, including two thermostats, one for controlling the heat applied to the water during brewing, and one for controlling the considerably higher heat applied to the water during the production of steam for milk-frothing.

External Elements. The external features mimic the features of the large caffè machines. They include: (D) an opening for servicing the water reservoir; (E) a gauge to indicate water level in the reservoir; (F) the brewing group, into which the filter holder clamps; (G) the filter holder and filter basket; (H) the steam wand or pipe; (I) the steam nozzle used to froth milk; (K) the controls, usually including a power switch and switches that activate the brewing and steam functions; and (L) the drip tray. Some designs, like the one pictured, also may include a cup-warming shelf atop the machine (M) and a built-in tamper (N).

Fully Automatic Machines. Some home pump machines brew coffee automatically, at the touch of a button. See page 116 for an illustration of such a machine. A series of mechanisms inside the machine grind the coffee, load it, tamp it, press the appropriate volume of water through the ground coffee, and finally drop the spent grounds into a removable waste container, all at the touch of a button. For drinks with frothed milk the operator still must froth the milk and assemble the drink, however.

Pod-Capable and Pod-Only Machines. In an effort to simplify the espresso brewing process manufacturers have developed home machines that give users the option of using small teabag-like individual servings of pre-ground coffee called pods. The most radical of these machines use special proprietary pods, which means you must buy your coffee for the life of your machine from the same people who manufactured it. Other, *ESE-standard,* machines use any pod that follows the widely adopted ESE standard, obviously an advantage in terms of price and range of choice. The ESE machines also typically offer the option of using either pods or conventional brewing procedure.

Typical home piston machine

CATEGORY 4 Countertop Piston Machines

- *With valve for frothing and heating milk*
- *Hand-operated piston controls coffee output*
- *Brewing pressure supplied by spring-loaded or hand-operated piston. Brewing pressure supplied by the piston will vary, but will considerably exceed the pressure supplied by trapped steam in the category 1 and 2 devices*

Advantages. Make near caffè-quality espresso and espresso drinks with frothed milk if used correctly; sturdier in construction than all but the most expensive category 3 machines; more conversation-provoking in appearance and operation than category 3 machines; offer more finely tuned control of brewing pressure than category 3 machines.

Disadvantages. Take up counter space; expensive; slower to warm up than category 3 machines; must be turned off and bled of steam pressure before refilling; boiler is exposed in most machines, and hot to the touch; manual piston designs may not provide as strong a brewing pressure as category 3 machines.

The sometimes hard-to-find machines in this category are piston devices, in which the additional pressure applied to the brewing water is delivered by a piston fitted into a cylinder, much as it is in the large piston machines still in use in many North American caffès. The piston is lifted, drawing water into the cylinder under the piston and above the bed of ground coffee, then depressed, pressing the water down through the coffee.

At least two currently available machines in this category incorporate a spring-loaded piston similar in design to the large manual caffè machines. A lever is depressed, compressing a spring above the piston; the spring then presses piston and water down, while the lever handle slowly returns to its original upright position. See page 119 for a cross-section illustration of such a mechanism.

However, most of the machines available in this category, including the widely available Pavoni Europiccola use the simple muscle power of the operator to provide the brewing pressure on the water. See the illustration on the right showing a cross-section of a typical manual piston machine. You raise the lever (A), drawing water from the boiler (B) into the cylinder (C). Next you lean on the lever, forcing the piston (D) down, and the brewing water through the filter holder and coffee at (E). Steam for milk frothing is provided by tapping the top of the boiler with the usual wand and valve (F).

Unlike the pump machines in category 3, these designs hold the water for both milk-frothing and coffee-brewing in the same large reservoir. This arrangement involves a couple of drawbacks. First, you need to wait for the entire reservoir to heat up before beginning to brew, a procedure that may take up to five minutes. Second, you must cool the entire machine before refilling the water reservoir. The pump machines in category 4 can be refilled while in use.

The great advantages to these machines are their solid construction and romantic appearance. Some aficionados also prefer to apply manual pressure to the brewing water because they can fine-tune the brewing pressure to compensate for variations in fineness of grind and the effects of humidity on the resistance of the coffee.

Home piston machines are often difficult to find. If you need help identifying a supplier, see Sources.

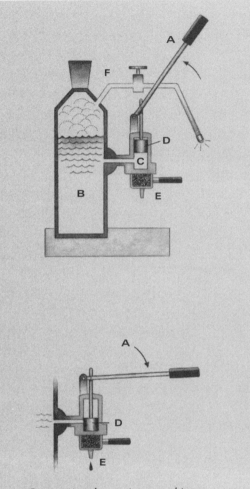

Cross-section, home piston machine

9 ESPRESSO AT HOME

PRODUCING THE DRINKS

A look at the list of beverages in the classic and contemporary American espresso cuisines given on pages 40–47 is an excellent place to start in assembling drinks at home. Remember, however, that much of the jargon attached to the various caffè drinks may be irrelevant in your kitchen, where the goal is simply to produce something you and your guests will enjoy, regardless of what it is called.

Before assembling espresso drinks, you may wish to look through the Espresso Breaks on selecting coffee (pages 89–92), brewing the coffee (pages 141–45), and frothing the milk (pages 141–52).

INGREDIENTS AND RECEPTACLES

Milk. Classic espresso cuisine uses whole milk for drinks like cappuccino and caffè latte. However, North Americans have pressed virtually every other liquid dairy and pseudo-dairy product into use: nonfat milk, 1 percent milk, 2 percent milk, extrarich milk, half and half, whipping cream, chocolate-flavored milk, soy milk, and (seasonally one hopes) commercial eggnog. With the proper technique, all will froth nicely, though the fattier versions of milk may be somewhat easier to froth for beginners using standard apparatus. To my taste, skim milk is too watery, and whipping cream too flat and fatty-tasting for the espresso cuisine. I suggest you try whole or 2 percent milk first and work your way up or down in fat content from there.

Whipped Cream. The whipped cream used in the best North American and Italian caffès is never canned and seldom sweetened. A generous dollop of it is laid on top of the drink. Customers then sweeten to taste. I suggest you begin as the caffès do, with proper whipped cream, unsweetened. You can always turn to substitutes for reasons of diet or convenience later, after you have experienced the basic cuisine.

Flavorings and Garnishes

The main flavorings used in espresso cuisine can be usefully divided into three categories:

- Traditional, "natural" flavorings used in the classic cuisine: the lemon peel in espresso Romano and the chocolate concentrate in a "real" caffè mocha, for example.
- Various garnishes sprinkled over frothed milk: in the traditional cuisine unsweetened chocolate and possibly cinnamon, but in the contemporary North American cuisine a variety of other powders and spices, some sweetened and some not.
- Italian-style syrups originally designed to flavor soft drinks, but increasingly used to flavor caffè latte and other espresso drinks made with frothed milk.

Flavorings in the Traditional Cuisines. The only flavorings the traditional espresso cuisines propose are simple to the point of austerity: a twist of lemon peel with straight espresso (*espresso Romano*), a dash of unsweetened chocolate powder over the frothed milk of a cappuccino, or a serving of concentrated hot chocolate in the Italian-American caffè mocha. In wildly experimental moments, the purist may substitute a twist of orange or tangerine peel for the lemon, or sprinkle cinnamon instead of chocolate on a cappuccino.

The chocolate powder used in the traditional cuisine should be unsweetened but as powerful and perfumy as possible. Most coffee specialty stores now sell a good version of this ingredient. A recipe for the concentrated hot chocolate used in the traditional caffè mocha is given later in this chapter under the heading for the drink.

Garnishes. Garnishes sprinkled over the head of frothed milk that covers the surfaces of drinks like cappuccino and caffè latte have become a ubiquitous part of North American espresso cuisine. They originated with the Italian practice of garnishing cappuccino with a light dusting of unsweetened chocolate powder, but North Americans now have extended the practice to include most drinks made with frothed milk and an increasing variety of powdered and grated spices and flavorings.

The unsweetened chocolate of the Italian cuisine is often replaced by a sweetened chocolate, for example, and some use Mexican chocolate, a sweetened, spiced chocolate sold in cake form that must be grated over the frothed milk. Still others prefer to grate or shave baking chocolate—unsweetened, semisweet, or white—over their frothed milk drinks. A good cheese grater works well.

To my knowledge cinnamon is never used in Italy to garnish coffee. It has a long history in North American spiced coffee drinks, however, so it inevitably made an early appearance as a garnish in the American espresso cuisine. For my part, I don't like cinnamon with espresso; I find that it doesn't harmonize with the dark tones of the coffee.

Like everything else about the exuberant contemporary American espresso cuisine, garnishes know no limits. At a Seattle espresso cart I once counted twelve garnishes available for patrons to sprinkle over their frothed-milk drinks, including sweetened and unsweetened chocolate powders, vanilla powder, orange powder, cinnamon, powdered nutmeg, and fresh nutmeg (presented with grater). The cart owner claimed that one man used every one of these garnishes on his caffè latte. Garnish madness appears to have peaked, however. Most Seattle espresso establishments now restrict themselves to chocolate, vanilla, cinnamon, and nutmeg. Of the various exotic garnishes I've tried the only one that has impressed me is the unsweetened vanilla powder, but if you like variety carry on.

Flavored Syrups. It was inevitable that the Italian-style fountain syrups that for so many years spread their tantalizing rainbow of colors and flavors across the back bars of caffès would break out of their limited role as soft-drink flavors and begin to find their way into coffee drinks. They are usually used to flavor tall, milky drinks rather than straight espresso, where more subtlety is called for. The flavored caffè latte in particular has become an American staple: Italian-style syrups are added to a freshly brewed caffè latte, making it a hazelnut latte, a raspberry latte, and on into the multiflavored latte sunset. Several brands of flavored syrup, made in both the United States and Europe, now compete with the widely distributed

Torani line. The all-natural Monin line has a reputation for subtlety, the Torani for energetic directness. If you try one of these syrups at home, keep in mind that they sweeten as well as flavor. If you are a sweet-loving sugar avoider, try one of the sugar-free syrups put out by DaVinci and others. DaVinci also offers all-natural-ingredients syrups. Currently the most popular flavors for coffee drinks are vanilla, hazelnut, Irish creme, and amaretto. If you have trouble finding syrups retail, consult Sources.

Serving Receptacles and other Accessories

Each of the traditional espresso drinks has a preferred serving receptacle. They are specified later in this chapter in the descriptions of the various drinks.

In Italy, espresso is almost never dispensed into plastic foam or cardboard. Such materials kill the delicate perfume of straight espresso. Rather than carrying their coffee back to work with them, Italians usually down a quick one standing at the bar, then fire off to work from there. This practice reflects the "small, powerful, perfect" aesthetic of Italian espresso cuisine.

Elegantly clad waiters and gofers can be seen hurrying through the business districts of large Italian cities carrying espresso drinks on trays, but these drinks are almost always dispensed into miniature insulated cups provided by the business person who is about to receive the coffee from his or her favorite bar. These little covered, insulated cups are usually made of metal, and are refined expressions of the designer's art.

Classic, heavy demitasse and cappuccino cups and matching saucers, together with the tall, 16-ounce glasses used in most North American caffès for caffè latte, can be found at near wholesale prices in restaurant supply stores. Such places also carry inexpensive demitasse spoons and long "iced tea" spoons to match the tall caffè latte glasses. More expensive, more distinctive, and often more fragile versions of these specialized receptacles and utensils are sold in kitchenware and specialty coffee stores, catalogs, and websites. Some sellers also may carry glass or ceramic bowls reminiscent of those used to serve caffè latte in Italian-American caffès during earlier decades.

Small to medium-sized stainless steel pitchers appropriate for frothing milk are useful but not essential. (You can froth milk in a large ceramic mug, for example.) A good frothing pitcher is light in weight, open at the top, with a broad pouring lip to facilitate coaxing frothed milk from pitcher to cup. If you buy such a pitcher, make certain that it fits easily under the steam wand of your espresso brewer.

Thermometers that clip on the side of frothing pitchers to assist in monitoring the exact heat of the milk under the froth are useful for beginners. I discuss these devices in more detail on pages 112–13.

Knock-out boxes like those used by small restaurants and caffès to bang the spent grounds out of the filter in preparation for the next dose of coffee may be useful for those who entertain a good deal or who wish to professionalize their espresso habit. A waste container with a solid edge works almost as well, but isn't nearly as elegant.

A jigger, or bartenders' shot glass marked at 1¼

ounces, is useful when brewing with pump and piston machines. Since the connoisseur's single serving of espresso should not exceed 1¼ ounces, the shot glass keeps you honest. And if you want to cut your serving short at an ounce or less, the transparent glass with measuring mark also facilitates that act of aesthetic restraint. When working at the more baroque end of espresso practice, use these glasses to measure syrups for flavored caffè lattes and similar extravagances.

Tampers, the little devices used to level and compress ground coffee in the filters of pump and piston machines, always come with the machines, but some aficionados become as involved with their tampers as cooks become with their knives, and buy fancy tampers made of metal and precious wood.

All such equipment can be purchased at most larger specialty stores, including the ubiquitous Starbucks, and on the Internet. See Resources.

TRADITIONAL CUISINE AT HOME

Straight Espresso

If you are after the perfection of straight espresso at home, you need to purchase a small pump or manual lever machine (categories 3 or 4, pages 106–12). Brewing devices that work by steam pressure alone, like those in category 2, pages 106–7, will make authentic espresso drinks with milk, but at best produce a flavorful but thin-bodied imitation of the unadorned drink. A perfectly pressed espresso exits the filter holder in majestic deliberation, all heavy golden froth that only gradually condenses into a dark, rich liquid as it gathers in the cup. Such results can only be gotten with good technique on machines that exert more than the relatively feeble pressure generated by the steam-only devices in categories 1 and 2.

Once you have mastered the brewing routine (see pages 141–45), the next step in making straight espresso the way you like it is to experiment with blend and roast (see Chapter 6). If your espresso tastes too sharp, try lighter-roast blends of sweeter coffees until you find one that suits you. If your espresso lacks punch try and a darker-roast blend. If you crave still more sharpness try a dark blend of higher-grown coffees like Guatemalas, Costa Ricas, or Kenyas.

Sweeteners and Flavorings. Don't feel reluctant to add sugar to straighten espresso for reasons of sophistication, by the way. Italians almost universally sweeten espresso, and the prejudice against adding sugar to coffee is one of those Puritan tics peculiar to some North Americans.

Some of the finest espresso blends are so naturally sweet (particularly those based on the finest Brazil coffees) that they can be drunk quite comfortably black. In terms of taste, the best sweetener for straight espresso is probably raw or demerara sugars. Honey tends to lose its sweetness when added to coffee.

Crema. Crema, the golden froth that mists over the surface of a well-made straight espresso and the subject of mystical rhapsodies by Italian espresso lovers, can present a problem for home brewing aficionados. You can consistently achieve it only with the pump and piston machines in categories 3 and 4, pages

107–12. If you own such a machine, and brew carefully, following the prescriptions on pages 141–45, your espresso should display the rich flavor and heavy body of the true product, together with at least some crema. If your espresso tastes good but you're not getting enough crema to make you happy, consult the relevant Espresso Break, pages 145–47, for some advice.

Receptacles. Straight espresso is traditionally served in a three-ounce cup (*demitasse,* French; *tazzina,* Italian), with appropriately proportioned spoon and saucer. To serve a single shot of espresso in anything except a small porcelain cup is like serving a fine wine in a jelly glass. Only a little less aesthetically disturbing is destroying the harmonic proportions of the espresso ensemble by serving a normal teaspoon on or next to the properly tiny cup and saucer. Everything about the Italian espresso ritual is focused on the satisfaction of a perfect moment that flawlessly fuses taste and gesture.

The tazzina must be warm when the coffee is pressed into it or the heavy cup will excessively cool the delicate coffee. Some home pump machines provide cup warming shelves, and with others the top of the machine can be used to keep cups warm regardless of the designers' intention. Hot steam from the steam wand or a little hot water run from the brew head can also be used to warm cups.

Straight Espresso Variations

The normal serving size for a true aficionado's espresso is about one-third to one-half the volume of a three-ounce demitasse, or 1¼ to 1½ ounces. *Corto, short,* or *short pull* means an espresso cut short at no more than one ounce. *Lungo, long,* or *long pull* refers to an espresso that almost completely fills the three-ounce demitasse. In both cases, the amount of ground coffee filling the filter basket should be the same; i.e. one dose, or about two level or one heaping tablespoons. The difference is the amount of water you allow to run through the coffee.

Espresso Romano is a normal serving of espresso with a twist of lemon on the side. You rub the outer surface of the lemon peel around the edge of the tiny cup so as to lightly and exquisitely scent the espresso as you drink it. The lemon paradoxically causes the espresso to taste sweeter, making the Romano a good choice for subtle, sugar-avoiding palates. Variations on the Romano replace the lemon peel with orange or tangerine.

Doppio or **double espresso** is simply two servings of espresso, brewed with two servings of ground coffee. The doppio, properly made, should fill only one-third to two-thirds of a 6-ounce cup with rich, creamy espresso. The suicidal *triple espresso* is simply a nearly full 6-ounce cup of espresso made with three servings of ground coffee. Since most home machines do not provide triple-sized filter baskets, those fools who might be tempted to drink a triple at home need to make it with two successive pulls.

For the *Americano,* essentially a North American–style, filter-strength coffee made by diluting a serving of espresso with several ounces of hot water, see the section on the new American cuisine below.

Assembling Simple Drinks with Frothed Milk

The distinctions among the various classic caffè drinks involving coffee and hot milk described on pages 128–30—cappuccino, latte macchiato, caffè latte, etc.—may seem a bit arbitrary. After all, the only actual differences are simple: the proportion of espresso to milk, the texture of the froth, how the milk and coffee are combined, and the kind of receptacle used.

However, I can vouch for the fact that these seemingly insignificant differences in procedure and presentation make for rather dramatic differences in taste among the various traditional drinks. So even though the distinctions among the various espresso-milk drinks may blur when you are making them at home, it is well to understand the gustatory goals behind these differences.

Here is a summary of the traditional coffee-milk drinks:

Espresso macchiato. Espresso "marked" with frothed milk. Adds the slightest topping of hot frothed milk to a tazzina of espresso. Here the espresso comes through in its full-bodied, sweetly pungent completeness; the milk barely mellows the bite of the coffee. An excellent way to take espresso for those who avoid sugar, but want the power of unadorned espresso. Good also after dinner, when a milkier drink like a cappuccino tastes too diffused and looks unsophisticated. Like straight espresso, served in a preheated 3-ounce demitasse.

Cappuccino. This is the prince (or princess) of espresso drinks made with milk. It is traditionally served in a 6-ounce cup, and the frothed milk is *added to the coffee in the cup.* The emphasis is on the froth rather than on the milk. A proper cappuccino is made with more milk than an espresso macchiato, but less than a latte macchiato, and considerably less than a caffè latte.

If a cappuccino is made correctly, the perfume and body of the espresso completely permeate the froth and milk, extending throughout the drink without losing a molecule of power, while the sharpness of the coffee is softened without being subdued. By comparison, the ubiquitous North American "latte" is milky, feeble, and insipid. However, few are the cappuccinos that are made correctly. Italian espresso blends are made to be drunk straight, so the Italian cappuccino is usually too bland. On the other hand, the North American cappuccino is usually bitter. The beans have been overroasted, the coffee overextracted, and the milk has been frothed too stiffly, so that it floats to the top of the espresso rather than subtly uniting with it.

Even made incorrectly, the cappuccino is a pleasant drink. But made correctly, it is an experience that turns ordinary coffee drinkers into obsessives, searching the world, or at least their neighborhoods, for a good cappuccino, and even reading entire books like this one to find the secret of how to assemble one at home.

Secrets of the Cappuccino. Here is how to produce an authentic cappuccino at home. Make a perfectly pressed, very rich, *small* quantity of espresso, 1 to 2 ounces, no more. Use a pump or piston machine if possible, and follow the instructions for pressing coffee on pages 141–44 as precisely as possible. Use a good North American espresso blend, medium-dark brown but not blackish, with oil just beginning to appear on the surface of the bean. Press the coffee into a warm 6-ounce cup.

Froth the milk to the point that it is still dense and a bit soupy, full of many tiny bubbles rather than a relatively few large ones. It should barely peak if you move a spoon through it. It should *not* stand up puffily. It should be hot, but not scalding. See pages 147–52 for instructions on frothing milk.

Pour the frothed milk into the cup. If you have frothed the milk correctly, and if you are using a thin-edged metal pitcher, the milk and froth should move together into the cup. You may need to encourage the froth with a spoon, however. The milk should not (cannot if it is frothed correctly) stand up like meringue above the top edge of the cup. A visual mark that you have done everything correctly is a brilliant white oval or heart shape on the surface of the drink, surrounded on all sides by a ring of dark brown, created by the espresso crema that has been carried to the surface of the milk.

Obviously, such precision does not come with your first home cappuccino. But if you have some idea what you are trying to achieve, your very first attempts should taste better than the production of most North American caffès.

Latte macchiato. The opposite of *espresso macchiato*, in that the milk "marks" the espresso rather than espresso marking the milk. There is not a great difference between espresso macchiato and caffè latte. Certainly made at home the two drinks will tend to overlap. With the latte macchiato the espresso is poured into a medium-sized glass of hot milk. The emphasis is on the milk, not the foam, and the coffee, when dribbled into the glass, tends to stain the milk in gradations, all contrasting with the modest white head of froth. The latte macchiato is a breakfast or early-day drink. It is the Italian version of the North American caffè latte.

Obviously the better and richer the espresso, the better the latte macchiato, but crema is irrelevant, and you can get away with espresso that is flavorful but somewhat light-bodied, the kind you can achieve with the modest steam-pressure machines described in category 2, pages 106–7. The sharp-flavored, oily, darkish roasts preferred by many North American caffès and roasters come into their own in the latte macchiato and caffè latte. The sharp flavor penetrates the milk better than the more rounded, sweeter roasts and blends that are appropriate for straight espresso.

The Italian macchiato is made with 1 to 2 ounces of well-brewed espresso, dribbled into about 5 ounces or so of hot milk, topped with froth in an 8-ounce glass. But the exact proportions hardly matter. The essential idea is hot milk, coffee, a little froth, and a tall-ish glass.

Caffè latte. The caffè latte dilutes the espresso in even more milk, in a taller glass or a bowl, with the espresso and milk poured simultaneously into the glass or bowl. The latte is definitely a breakfast drink. The essential idea is to provide something to dip your breakfast roll into and enough liquid to wash the roll down with afterward. As with the latte macchiato, the head of froth is usually modest, so as not to interfere with the roll-dipping operation and not to distract from the psychological sensation of virtually bathing in hot, milky liquid.

The North American latte usually combines one longish serving (about 1½ ounces) of espresso with enough milk to fill a 12- to 16-ounce glass. This recipe produces a weak, milky drink, and has encouraged various customizations involving less milk and more espresso. A terminology has evolved that permits the espresso bar customer to specify both number of servings of espresso (*single, double, triple,* or *quad,* or four) and volume of milk (*small* or *short,* or enough milk to fill an 8-ounce container; *tall,* enough to fill a 14-ounce container; or various pop terms like *grande,* 16 ounces, *venti* (Starbucks), or *mondo,* enough to fill 20 to 24 ounces). Thus a latte can range from a powerful drink with three servings of espresso and only a few ounces of milk to a drink in which a single serving of espresso barely flavors a virtual kindergarten class's worth of hot milk.

Obviously all of this terminology has little application to assembling a caffè latte at home. You experiment with the proportions of milk to coffee until you arrive at a satisfying balance. Most people customize the proportions to suit the moment: They may crave a stronger or a weaker drink depending on the time of day and the current state of their nervous systems and work schedule.

The standard receptacle in the United States for the caffè latte is the plain, 16-ounce tapered restaurant glass used in other contexts for serving everything from milkshakes to beer. A more interesting and, arguably more authentic, serving receptacle for the caffè latte is a relatively deep 12- to 16-ounce ceramic or glass bowl.

Traditional Caffè Mocha

Next to the cappuccino, the caffè mocha is probably the most abused drink in the traditional espresso cuisine. The classic Italian-American caffè mocha combines an American-sized serving (1 to 2 ounces) of espresso and perhaps 2 ounces of *strong,* usually *unsweetneed* hot chocolate in a tallish 8-ounce ceramic mug, topped with hot milk and froth. The drink is sweetened to taste after it has been assembled and served, just as with any other espresso beverage. This drink, smoothly perfumy and powerful, has been turned into a sort of hot milkshake by most North American caffès. Operators essentially make a caffè latte with a dollop of chocolate fountain syrup in it. With a true mocha the chocolate flavor is true, deep, and strong; it permeates the froth and roars down your throat playing a sort of tantalizing tag with the taste of the equally powerful espresso.

The only trick to making the counterfeit caffè mocha at home is combining the chocolate syrup with the espresso before you pour in the milk. Use any good chocolate fountain syrup and adjust the volume of syrup and milk to taste. Those who are interested in experimenting with the classic caffè mocha will need to make a chocolate concentrate. One part unsweetened, dark chocolate powder mixed with two parts hot water makes an authentic version of this concentrate. The powder and water can be combined while heating them with the steam wand of the espresso machine. As you direct the steam into the water and chocolate, stir with a spoon or small whisk, working the floating gobs of dry chocolate down into the gradually heating water. Either sweeten the mixture to taste when you mix it (try brown or demerara sugar), or leave it unsweetened, giving you and your guests an opportunity to sweeten the assembled drink after it has been served. If you prefer a lighter-tasting concentrate, add a few drops of vanilla extract to the mix while you are heating it. Try about ¼ teaspoon to every cup of chocolate powder, adjusting to taste.

To make the classic caffè mocha, combine about 2 ounces of this concentrate with one serving (1¼ ounces) of espresso and enough hot, frothed milk to fill an 8- to 10-ounce mug. Vary the proportions of chocolate, espresso, milk, and froth to taste.

Once mixed, by the way, the chocolate concentrate can be stored in a capped jar in the refrigerator for up to three weeks. The mixture may separate; when you are ready to use the concentrate, invert and shake the jar, then pour out into a frothing pitcher or mug as much concentrate as you wish to consume, and reheat it, using the steam wand.

Some caffès now use a white-chocolate concentrate to produce special espresso drinks with names like White-Chocolate Mocha, Mocha Bianca, etc. To make an authentic white-chocolate concentrate melt in a double boiler approximately 2 ounces sweetened white baking chocolate in ½ cup boiling water. Bring the mixture to a boil, then reduce heat to a low bubbling boil for about 3 minutes, stirring regularly. This concentrate also can be refrigerated for up to three weeks. Substitute it for the chocolate concentrate in caffè mocha and other chocolate-espresso-frothed milk drinks. It contributes a sweet, delicately flavored chocolate component to the drink. Torani and DaVinci both produce a pre-made white chocolate syrup that can be ordered through their respective websites. See Sources.

Both of the made-from-scratch chocolate concentrates can be used to make hot chocolate drinks without espresso. Simply combine the concentrate to taste with hot frothed milk.

POSTMODERN CUISINE AT HOME

Contemporary American cuisine brings an exuberant sense of experiment to espresso tradition. Most of its innovations can be duplicated easily at home.

Adding Flavors

The ingredients section leading off this chapter describes the various classes of flavorings in the new North American espresso cuisine. Making use of these flavorings at home could not be simpler: merely add Italian-style fountain syrup to taste or as indicated below to your favorite drink. See page 133 for more on choosing syrups and Sources for suggestions on where to buy them.

Here are some suggestions for specific drinks.

Flavored Caffè Latte. If you make your caffè latte in a 12-ounce glass, start with ½ to 1 ounce of syrup to one serving (1¼ ounces) of espresso and about 8 ounces of hot frothed milk. Put the syrup in the glass, add the freshly pulled espresso, mix the espresso and syrup lightly, then add the frothed milk. Adding the syrup last, after the milk, tends to dull the drink. Nut flavors (amaretto, orgeat/almond, hazelnut) and spice (vanilla, anisette, crème de menthe, chocolate mint) are good places to start with your syrup experiments. Berry flavors are attractive, but most tropical fruit and soda fountain flavors (root beer, etc.) seem not to resonate well with coffee.

Flavored Cappuccino. Go very lightly with the syrup here, ¼ to ½ ounce at the most, or you may ruin the balance of the drink. Make a classic cappuccino (see page 128). Add the syrup to the espresso, mix lightly, and add the milk. If you enjoy visual drama, try applying a thin, moving dribble of syrup across the surface of the froth, creating an attractive pattern (or creatively messing up the counter).

Flavored Caffè Mocha. Make a classic mocha (see pages 130–31), adding a dash of hazelnut, almond, orange, or mint syrup mixed in with the chocolate syrup.

For still further extravagances, see the section on Soda Fountain Espresso at Home: Hot Drinks (page 133), and Cold Drinks (pages 135–36).

Garnishes: The traditional garnishes (unsweetened chocolate, cinnamon, grated nutmeg, and grated orange peel) are now augmented by an array of sweetened and unsweetened garnishing powders put out by various firms and marketed in fancy food and specialty coffee stores. See page 172. If you combine one flavor of syrup and another of garnish you have an opportunity to either subtly delight the palate or grossly confuse it. Flavor combinations that seem to marry well with espresso are orange and chocolate, almond and chocolate, hazelnut and chocolate, mint and chocolate, and orange and vanilla. Make the syrup one choice and the garnish the other. Specialty coffee stores usually sell the classic garnishes, and others can be found in the spice section of large supermarkets.

Coffeeless Espresso Cuisine

So long as you have the machine, the garnishes, the milk and the syrups, you might consider some espresso cuisine without the espresso.

Flavored Frothed Milk. This drink appears in caffès under a variety of names, from the no-nonsense "Steamer" to the fanciful "Moo." Add frothed milk to syrup (start with ½ to 1 ounces syrup per 8 ounces milk) and mix.

Hot Chocolate, Cioccolata. Make a chocolate concentrate (see page 131), and top 3 to 4 ounces of hot concentrate with 4 to 5 ounces of hot frothed milk to fill an 8-ounce mug. Garnish with either chocolate powder, vanilla powder, grated orange peel, or shave white chocolate. Or simply stir chocolate fountain syrup to taste into milk while frothing it.

Hot Chocolate with Whipped Cream, Cioccolata con Panna. Halve the milk in the previous recipe and top with whipped cream, either unsweetened, sweetened, or flavored (for flavoring whipped cream see below).

Soda Fountain Espresso at Home: Hot Drinks

Once you have mastered the basic exclamatory vocabulary of syrups, frothed milk, espresso, and garnishes, you may want to add whipped cream to your repertoire. Add moderately stiff whipped cream (sweetened or unsweetened) to any espresso drink in place of a roughly similar volume of frothed milk. In other words, if you make a caffè mocha, omit about 2 ounces of frothed milk and replace it with a healthy dollop of whipped dream to fill the mug. Garnish the whipped cream as you would the frothed milk.

The Torani syrups company suggests flavored whipped cream. Blend 1 pint whipping cream with 3 to 4 ounces syrup. Store this sweetened, flavored whipped cream and use it as suggested above. Thus, if you're careful and don't get too dizzy with your choice of flavors, you can serve a caffè latte with milk and coffee augmented by one flavor and whipped cream by a second. And, of course, a dash of garnish to the whipped cream will complicate the business still further.

Try, for example, orange-flavored whipped cream on a classic caffè mocha; or simply vanilla-flavored whipped cream on straight espresso, with a garnish of chocolate powder. I won't tempt the ghost of espresso purists past with anything more complex than those rather modest suggestions—experiment. Maraschino whipped cream on a passion fruit–flavored cappuccino, garnished with orange peel? I hear Signor Gaggia rolling around from here.

Hybrid Drinks

Caffè Americano. The Americano is another innovation apparently developed in Seattle. It permits you to produce something resembling North American–style filter coffee on an espresso machine. The trick is to make a single 1-to-2-ounce serving of espresso, then *add hot water to taste.* If you simply run several ounces of hot water through a single dose of ground coffee, you will end up destroying the subtle aromatics of the espresso with the harsh-tasting chemicals that continue to be extracted from the coffee after it has given up its flavor oils. If, on the other hand, you make a 6-ounce cup of coffee with three doses of coffee you are simply delivering a triple espresso, rather than an Americano, which tries to keep the perfumes of the original espresso while extending them into a longer drink with hot water.

For those who like the fresh aromatics of espresso, but also crave the lightness and length of an North American–style filter coffee, the Americano, made correctly, is an excellent compromise. You can brew medium-roasted varietal coffees as well as dark-roasted coffees using the Americano method, and some Seattle caffès and carts do exactly that. They will brew an Ethiopia Harrar Americano, a Sumatra Americano, etc.

Depth Charge. Appropriately named for the sneaky underwater munitions famous in World War II for destroying submarines, this caffeine-underground invention drops a serving of espresso (tastes best made short, about 1 ounce) into a cup of regular drip coffee. Caffeine overload aside, this can be a very pleasant and complex drink, particularly when the drip coffee is freshly brewed (try a brightly floral coffee like an Ethiopia Yirgacheffe).

Iced Espresso Drinks

You can make almost any espresso drink iced. There are several principles to be observed in converting hot drink recipes to cold, however.

- Use cold milk rather than hot milk in iced cappuccino, caffè latte, etc., so as not to melt the ice prematurely, thus overly diluting the coffee. If you wish to provide a decorative head of froth to dress up the drink and provide a setting for garnishes, add a modest topping of hot froth (not milk) *after* you have combined the ice, coffee, and cold milk. Or use one of the pumping French-press milk-frothing devices described on pages 112–13 that produce a cold froth to start with.
- Espresso that has been brewed and then refrigerated will not make as flavorful a drink as freshly brewed hot espresso, but holds its strength better when poured over the ice. Take your choice.
- The home-mixed chocolate concentrate I recommend for the hot caffè mocha tends to separate in iced drinks. You may find a pre-mixed fountain syrup more satisfactory for a cold summer caffè mocha.

Latte Granita, Granita Latte, Frappuccino (Starbucks), Etc. Unlike straightforward iced espresso drinks, which are cold versions of the classic cuisine and sweetened to taste after serving, these are the slushy, sweet, partly frozen drinks served in caffès and espresso bars.

Caffès produce these drinks in one of two ways. The authentic approach involves combining freshly brewed espresso, milk, ice, sugar and (usually) vanilla in a high-powered commercial blender. This is the approach taken at Starbucks, Peet's, and many other quality-oriented chains and caffès. The less authentic approach combines pre-brewed espresso (or even a commercial espresso concentrate) with the other ingredients in machines that maintain the mixture at freezing temperature while agitating it to prevent it from solidifying.

In both cases the result is a pleasantly grainy beverage: sweet, milky, and refreshing, though sometimes cloying if the barista overdoes the sugar. The advantage to the blender approach is the freshly brewed coffee, plus the possibility of customizing the drink by request.

It is difficult to make a drink with quite the heavy, smooth yet grainy texture of the commercial latte granita using a home blender, but you can produce a very attractive drink, better flavored than most caffè productions, and tailored to suit your own tastes.

For each serving brew one serving (1¼ ounces) of full-strength espresso. While the espresso is still hot, dissolve in it 1 to 3 rounded teaspoons of sugar. One teaspoon produces an austere if seductive drink; three will probably satisfy those with a sweet tooth. Combine the sweetened espresso in a blender with about 2 ounces of cold milk and 3 ice cubes per serving (partly crushed), plus a few drops of vanilla extract. Blend until the ice is barely pulverized and still grainy; serve immediately. Experiment with the amount of milk, ice, espresso, sweetener, and vanilla until you obtain a custom balance that satisfies you. You can brew and sweeten the espresso in advance and store it in a stoppered jar in the refrigerator for convenience, although the longer you refrigerate it the slightly less flavorful your "latte granita" will be.

For a *mocha granita* dissolve ½ to 1 fluid ounce of chocolate fountain syrup in the freshly brewed espresso along with the sugar. Proceed as above. For every ½ ounce of chocolate syrup reduce the sugar by 1 teaspoon.

The Traditional Espresso Granita. The austerely rich, classic Italian-American granita, more a dessert than a beverage, has become difficult to find in the United States, having been upstaged by the more in-gratiating latte granita.

The classic granita consists of straight espresso that has been frozen and crushed, then served in a sundae dish topped with whipped cream. When eating it you combine the powerful espresso ice and the whipped cream in judiciously balanced spoonfuls.

For those who wish to experiment with this disappearing delicacy at home: Brew two doses of full-strength espresso per serving, freeze in an ice cube tray, then crush thoroughly before serving in a small-ish parfait or sundae dish. Top with lightly sweetened whipped cream dusted with chocolate powder.

Soda Fountain Espresso at Home: Cold Drinks

Espresso, cold milk, ice, flavored syrups, garnishes, ice cream, and whipped cream can be combined in a literally endless number of ways. Here are just a few suggestions.

Affogato. Pour one or two servings (the shorter the better) of espresso over vanilla ice cream. Either stop there and start eating, or top with whipped cream, flavored or unflavored, and garnish with grated chocolate, white or dark, chocolate powder, or grated orange peel.

Cappuccino and Ice Cream. Combine one serving (1¼ ounces) espresso with 4 ounces cold milk; lay in a scoop of vanilla, chocolate, or coffee ice cream. If you prefer, top with a dollop of whipped cream and a dash of garnish.

Espresso Fizz. Pour one serving (1¼ ounces) freshly brewed espresso in a tall 12-ounce glass; mix in sugar to taste (try 1 teaspoon); fill glass with ice and soda water. Serve without mixing so that the drama of the sugared espresso lurking at the bottom of the drink can be appreciated. Before drinking mix with an iced tea or soda spoon.

Espresso Egg Creme. Pour one serving (1¼ ounces) freshly brewed espresso in a tall 12-ounce glass; mix in sugar to taste (try 1 teaspoon). Add 1 ounce whole milk or half and half and fill glass with ice and soda water. Serve as in the previous recipe.

Mocha Egg Creme. Pour one serving (1¼ ounces) freshly brewed espresso in a tall 12-ounce glass; mix in ½ to 1 ounce commercial chocolate syrup. Add 1 ounce whole milk or half and half and fill glass with ice and soda water. Serve as in the previous recipes.

Italian Sodas. The syrups used in the contemporary American espresso cuisine were originally intended as soft-drink syrups. Combine 1 to 1½ ounces of one of these Italian-style syrups with ice and soda water to fill a tall 12-ounce glass. If you haven't already, try orgeat (almond) or tamarind. Garnish the tamarind with a slice of lemon.

Italian Egg Creme. Pour 1 ounce whole milk or half and half and 1 to 1½ ounces syrup in the bottom of a tall 12-ounce glass. Fill with ice and soda water.

Espresso Float. Make an espresso fizz or espresso egg creme with chilled soda water but without the ice; leave space at the top of a 12- or 16-ounce glass; add 1 or 2 scoops of any flavor ice cream.

Espresso Ice Cream Soda. Make an espresso float in a 16-ounce glass, leaving room at the top for whipped cream, flavored or unflavored, garnished with grated chocolate or orange peel.

CHAI, OR THE ESPRESSO MACHINE MEETS TEA

Traditionally, chai is a mixture of spices and black tea drunk with hot milk and honey in the Middle East, India, and Central Asia. The spice mix is usually boiled for fifteen or twenty minutes and combined with black tea brewed in the usual way. This liquid concentrate is then strained and mixed with hot milk and honey.

Some innovator in the American Northwest came up with the notion of making the milk component of traditional chai hot *frothed* milk. People in Oregon loved it, some of them anyhow. People in Washington and California loved it. Chai is now part of the repertoire of the new American espresso cuisine, usually as a tall, hot milk drink called a *chai latte*. The traditional black tea chai has been joined by various non-caffeinated herbal tea chais, usually mint-based.

The spices in traditional chai always include ginger, cinnamon, and cardamom, but may include smaller amounts of coriander, nutmeg, cloves, star anise, fennel, black pepper, and orange zest. Americans are wont to add vanilla to sweeten and mellow the mix, but vanilla is not a typical component in authentic chais. As the chai phenomena spreads it also attracts the kind of dubious culinary innovation that brought us instant coffee and white bread. Chai mixes are becoming easier and easier to use and tackier and tackier in taste. The latest powdered versions resemble a sort of Middle Eastern Kool-Aid.

The espresso machine owner interested in making chai at home has several alternatives. I present them in order from most authentic to least.

Most Authentic Chai. (Short of grinding the spices yourself.) From a natural foods store buy a dry chai mix that keeps the spice mix separate from the tea

(Marsala Chai is a good one) and prepare a liquid chai concentrate as described on the package. This involves boiling the spices (usually for about 20 minutes), removing the spice mix from the heat, adding black tea, steeping the tea in the spice mix for about 4 minutes, then straining the mixture. The resulting concentrate can be refrigerated for 2 to 3 weeks.

When you are ready for your chai latte, combine equal parts of frothed milk and the liquid chai concentrate. If you have refrigerated the chai concentrate, gently reheat it with the steam wand before combining it with the hot frothed milk. Sweeten with honey to taste. If in doubt start with 1 drippy, overflowing teaspoonful of honey per 6 to 8 ounces of the milk and chai combination.

Next Most Authentic Chai. Buy a chai mix from the refrigerator section of large natural foods stores. These chais are usually produced using the same procedure you would use at home, but often are sweetened with sugar syrup, which robs your chai of the authentic richness of the honey. Heat gently with the steam wand and mix as directed on the label with hot frothed milk.

Third Most Authentic Chai. Buy a liquid chai mix from the tea or coffee section of large natural foods stores. These chais, which do not require refrigeration, are liquid concentrates of varying degrees of authenticity using varying recipes. Most are sweetened with sugar syrup, some are not. Some include vanilla, some don't. You can only experiment.

Least Authentic Chai. I am not sure whether powdered instant chai mixes (just add hot milk and serve!) have made it to specialty foods shelves, but if they have, walk on by. Every one I have tasted is listless, sugary, and cloying.

ESPRESSO SERVICE AT HOME

Espresso cuisine has become so various in its manifestations that any group of guests is likely to include a mix of purists, Seattle-style postmodernists, and espresso innocents. Consequently, those readers who entertain in conventional fashion may wish to serve their espresso cuisine buffet style and allow their guests to doctor their espresso themselves. The garnishes, unsweetened flavorings, and Italian syrups described earlier in this chapter all have a long shelf life. The syrups in particular are attractively packaged, and look colorful in an array on a tray or buffet.

The do-it-yourself approach also can be extended to assembling the traditional milk and espresso drinks. Serve a largish pitcher of hot frothed milk, a smaller pitcher of fresh espresso, and perhaps a pitcher of freshly mixed Italian-style hot chocolate, unsweetened, with sugar on the side, and let your guests have their will with it all. Purists, of course, will justifiably want their demitasse of espresso or their cappuccino brewed into the cup and served fresh, but those latte lovers who order a double mint mocha or whatever will doubtless be happier wading in themselves.

ESPRESSO DRINKS FORTIFIED WITH SPIRITS

Although there are many traditional recipes that combine spirits with drip or filter coffee, by comparison there is little precedent for drinks that marry espresso with alcohol. Perhaps the concentrated nature of espresso discourages such experiments. With the addition of flavored caffè lattes and latte granitas to the cuisine, North American espresso culture seems to be drifting more toward soda fountain than saloon. This trend may be owing partly to coffee and tea's privileged position (along with red wine perhaps) as the only widely consumed intoxicants that have so far made it through the gauntlet of modern medical testing without being definitely implicated in any diseases. Perhaps by dissociating espresso from hard liquor, today's coffee culture is attempting to consolidate its position as the "nice vice" of the millennium.

Nevertheless, those adults whose vices remain nice but also versatile will find that spirits and liqueurs used with discretion make an attractive complement to espresso.

Espresso fortified with grappa is probably the most classic such combination. Italians sometimes call it *caffè corretto*. Any espresso drink can be lightly fortified with brandy, which complicates both the flavor and effect of the drink without overwhelming its essential nature. Dark rum, anise-flavored spirits like Pernot and ouzo, and bourbon whiskey also combine attractively with espresso. Many people add a tiny dollop of sweet liqueur to straight espresso after dinner in place of the usual sugar, thus both sweetening and flavoring the cup. In fact, some enthusiasts do a sort of coffee overload by making the liqueur a dark-roast, coffee-based liqueur like Kahlua. This combination (or intensification) of coffee on coffee is a bit much to my taste, but those who find that the palace of culinary wisdom lies along the road of excess may enjoy it.

Of course the purist will protest that one shouldn't mix good brandy or liqueur and good espresso, but should enjoy them separately, side by side. In a culture where caffè latte is flavored with chocolate mint syrup such objections seem a bit hypothetical.

Recipes for Fortified Espresso Drinks

Here are a few recipes that straightforwardly combine spirits and espresso, or at least make use of the unique capabilities of the espresso machine. Aside from the San Francisco cappuccino, they are all my own inventions, and usually represent traditional coffee-and-spirits recipes reinterpreted for the espresso cuisine.

San Francisco cappuccino is a traditional, yet curiously named drink, since it uses no espresso at all, but is a combination of hot chocolate, brandy, and frothed milk. Once a favorite of Italian-Americans and their bohemian associates in San Francisco, it has now virtually disappeared except at some old-time San Francisco bars like the wonderful Tosca in the North Beach neighborhood, where these brandy-chocolate drinks are still assembled using a pair of sixty-year-old Victoria Arduino espresso machines.

To create the San Francisco cappuccino at home, start by dissolving about 1 rounded teaspoon of unsweetened cocoa together with sugar to taste (1 rounded teaspoonful is traditional) in ½ ounce or so of hot water in a 6-ounce, stemmed glass of the heavy, flared variety designed for Irish coffee. You can use the steam wand of your espresso brewer to heat the combination as you mix it. Add 1 jigger (1½ ounces) of brandy, mix, and top with about 3 ounces of hot, soupily frothed milk, or enough to fill the glass. If you are dubious about the sugar part of the drink you can assemble the drink without sweetening it, and add sugar or other sweetener to taste after assembling the drink.

For *Espresso Gloria* (my name for a drink based on the traditional recipe for Coffee Gloria) combine 1 serving (1¼ ounces) of freshly-brewed espresso, about 3 ounces of hot water, 1 jigger of brandy, and granulated or brown sugar to taste (1 teaspoonful is traditional). Follow the same recipe, substituting Calvados, or apple brandy, for the grape brandy, and this drink becomes *Espresso Normandy.* To make it taste even more like northern France, use a darker-roast coffee than usual (the nearly black style that is usually sold as Dark French) when brewing the espresso.

Many traditional coffee drinks add a head of lightly whipped cream to sweetened, fortified coffee. A good variation on the whipped cream, spirits, and coffee theme for the espresso lover might be called Venetian Espresso, after the similarly named and constructed traditional drink, Venetian Coffee.

For *Venetian Espresso* place sugar to taste (1 rounded teaspoonful is traditional) in a 6-ounce, stemmed glass of the heavy, flared variety designed for Irish coffee. Brew one medium-to-long serving (1½ to 2 ounces) of espresso per glass, and pour over the sugar. Add 1 jigger of brandy and stir. Top with whipping cream that has been beaten until it is partly stiff, but still pours. The whipping cream should be soft enough to float with an even line on the surface of the coffee, rather than bob around in lumps. If the cream tends to sink or mix with the coffee, pour it into a teaspoon held just at the surface of the coffee. Once the whipped cream has been added this drink should not be stirred. Sip the hot coffee and brandy through the cool whipped cream. Made with crème de cacao this drink could plausibly be called *Espresso Cacao.* Other spirits also work well: bourbon, rum, Strega, Calvados, grappa, and almost any liqueur, including (for espresso overload lovers) dark-roast coffee liqueurs like Kahlua.

Espresso Brûlot Diabolique, Espresso Brûlot, Espresso Diable, and *Espresso Flambè* are all plausible names for a theatrical drink in which a flavored brandy mixture is heated, ignited, and combined with espresso. For each cup assemble one serving (1¼ ounces) of freshly brewed espresso, about 2 ounces of hot water, 1½ jiggers of brandy, granulated or brown sugar to taste (1 teaspoonful per cup is traditional), 1 large strip orange peel, 1 small strip lemon peel, and 8 whole cloves.

Warm the sugar, brandy, cloves, and orange and lemon peels in a chafing dish. Stir gently to dissolve the sugar. Place one serving espresso and 2 ounces hot water in each cup or glass, and place around the chafing dish. When the brandy mixture has been gently warmed (you should be able to smell the brandy very clearly from three feet away if it's ready), pass a lighted match over the chafing dish. The brandy should ignite. If it doesn't, it probably is not warm enough. Let the brandy burn for as long as you get a reaction from your audience (but not over half a minute), then ladle over the coffee. The flame will usually die when the brandy is ladled into the glasses. Don't let the brandy burn too long, or the flame will consume all of the alcohol.

If you don't have a chafing dish, put the sugar in each glass before you add the coffee; heat the brandy, cloves, and citrus on the stove. When the fumes are rising, pour into a fancy bowl and bring to the table. Carefully lay an ounce or two of the brandy mixture atop each glass of coffee; if you pour the brandy gently it will float on the surface of the coffee. To ignite the brandy, pass a match over each glass; to douse the flame, mix the brandy and coffee.

If you have trouble getting the brandy to float, try holding a teaspoon on the surface of the coffee and pouring the brandy mixture onto the spoon, letting it spread from there over the coffee. Also remember to add the sugar to the coffee, not to the brandy mixture, or the sugar will make the brandy too heavy to float.

The same drink is good made with dark rum. Follow the preceding instructions, substituting rum for brandy and omitting the flaming process. Another possibility is to use half rum and half brandy.

ESPRESSO BREAK

BREWING THE COFFEE

Note: The instructions that follow are meant to elaborate and complement those provided by the manufacturer of your espresso brewer. Be certain you have read and understood the safeguards, cautions, and instructions that accompany your brewing device before supplementing them with the advice and encouragement given below.

Coffee and Roast. Classic espresso is brewed using a coffee roasted medium-dark-to-dark brown, but not black. This roast usually is called *espresso* or *Italian* in stores, but any coffee roasted to that color, no matter what it's called, will make a plausible espresso. Typically, however, blends designed especially for espresso blends make the best espresso beverages. They range from mild, sweet blends best for straight espresso, to dark, rich, pungent blends best for long milk drinks like caffè latte. See Chapter 6 and associated Espresso Break for more on choosing coffee for espresso brewing.

Always use at least as much coffee as is recommended by the manufacturer of your machine. Never use less. The usual measure for commercial machines is about two level tablespoons per serving. If in doubt, use two level tablespoons of finely ground coffee for every serving of espresso. In order to achieve a flavorful cup, you may have to use more. I find that with many home pump and piston machines a single serving of brewed espresso with the proper richness only can be ob-

tained by using the double filter basket rather than the single, and by loading it with a double dose of ground coffee.

Brewing Principles. There are two requirements for making good espresso. First, you must grind the coffee just fine enough, and tamp it down in the filter basket just firmly and uniformly enough, so that the barrier of ground coffee resists the pressure of the hot water sufficiently to produce a slow dribble of dark, rich liquid. Second, you need to stop the dribble at just the right moment, before the oils in the coffee are exhausted and the dark, rich dribble turns into a tasteless brown torrent.

Grind. The best grind for espresso is very fine and gritty, but not a dusty powder. If you look at the ground coffee from a foot away, you should barely be able to distinguish the particles. If you rub some between your fingers, it should feel gritty. If you have whole beans ground at a store, ask for a fine grind for an espresso machine. A fine, precise, uniform grind is particularly important for pump and piston machines, which demand an especially dense layer of coffee to resist their high brewing pressure. See Chapter 7 and below for more on grind and grinders for espresso brewing.

Preheating Group, Filter holder, and Cup. Servings of straight espresso are so small and delicate that everything

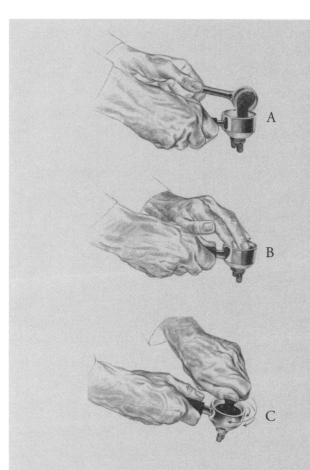

from the frothing wand into the cup. Those who drink their espresso with frothed milk can afford some carelessness in this regard. The hot milk usually manages to compensate lukewarm coffee and a cool cup.

Filling and Tamping. Different types of brewing devices have somewhat differing requirements for this important operation.

Filling and tamping for brewers and machines with external, caffè-style clamp-in filter and filter holder (categories 2 through 4): Fill the filter basket with coffee to the point indicated by the manufacturer, distributing it evenly in the filter basket (A). Then press the coffee down, exerting roughly similar pressure across the entire surface of the dose. *With machines that work by steam pressure alone* (category 2, pages 106–7) use your fingertips to consistently but *lightly* press the coffee across its entire surface (B). Don't hammer on it. *With pump and piston machines (categories 3 and 4, pages 107–12)* use the device called a *tamper* that was packaged with your machine, and exert strong pressure, decisively packing the coffee into the filter basket (C). As you tamp the coffee you might simultaneously twist the tamper, which *polishes* the surface of the coffee and assists in creating a uniform resistance to the brewing water.

Never use less than the minimum volume of ground coffee recommended for the machine, even if you are brewing a single cup. If the coffee gushes out rather than dribbling, compensate by using a finer grind or by tamping the coffee more firmly. If it still gushes out, use a bit more coffee and, if you

immediately surrounding the brewing act must be warmed in advance to preserve heat in the freshly-pressed coffee. If you have a pump or piston machine and are making your first cup, be sure to preheat the group, filter, and filter holder by running a small amount of hot brewing water through them. The demitasse into which you press the coffee should also be warm. Use the cup warmer on your machine, the top of your machine as an improvised cup warmer, or run some steam are grinding at home, increase the fineness of the grind. If the coffee oozes out rather than dribbling steadily, use a coarser grind or go easier on the tamping.

For pump and piston machines good brewing parameters can be described more precisely. Espresso from such high-powered machines tastes richest, sweetest, and most complete if each shot is limited in volume to one-and-one-half ounces and dribbles out of the filter holder in about 15 to 25 seconds after the first drop appears. If the shot gushes out in fewer than 15 seconds it is likely to be watery and thin tasting; more than 25 and it will taste burned and bitter.

A note on self-tamping machines and pods and capsules: Some pump machines have a *self-tamping* feature. The shower head on the underside of the group automatically compresses the coffee as you clamp the filter holder into the machine. You still need to use the tamper to assure that the coffee is evenly distributed in the filter basket, however. Machines that brew with pre-packaged, single-serving espresso pods or capsules require no loading or tamping. The pods or capsules are simply inserted into the special filter holder. With these machines you still must time the brewing accurately, however, to avoid ruining the espresso by running too much water through the ground coffee.

Filling and tamping for stovetop espresso brewers with internal filter baskets (most brewers in category 1, page 106): Most stovetop espresso brewers contain the ground coffee in a largish sleeve inside the device, rather than in a caffè-style filter unit that clamps to the outside. When using these stovetop devices with interior filter baskets, *do not tamp the*

If the coffee is ground too coarsely or packed too loosely, the brewed coffee will gush out in a pale torrent, top. *If ground too finely or packed too tightly, it will ooze out in dark, reluctant drops,* center. *If ground and packed correctly, it will issue out properly in a slow but steady, tapered dribble,* bottom.

coffee unless the instructions that come with your machine ask you to do so. Use the same fine grind as recommended above, use as much as the manufacturer's instructions recommend, distribute it evenly in the filter basket, and proceed. For stovetop machines with caffè-style filter holders that clamp to the outside of the machine, tamp lightly as described above.

Clamping the Filter Holder into the Group. Always wipe off any grains of coffee that may have clung to the edges of the filter holder. They may cause brewing water to leak around the edges of filter and dilute the coffee. Also make certain that the filter holder is firmly and evenly locked into the group. Until you get the knack of the clamping gesture, you may need to stoop over and peer under the group to make certain that the filter holder is evenly snugged in place.

Brewing. Timing is everything is espresso brewing. The richest and most flavorful coffee issues out at the very beginning. As brewing continues, the coffee becomes progressively thinner and more bitter. Consequently, *collect only as much coffee as you will actually serve.* If you are brewing one serving, cut off the flow of coffee after one serving has dribbled out, even if you have two servings of ground coffee in the filter basket. If you are brewing two servings, cut off the flow after two. And no matter how many servings you are trying to make, *never allow the coffee to bubble and gush into your serving carafe or cup.* Such thin, overextracted coffee will taste so bad that it's better to start over than to insult your palate or guests by serving it.

If you are using a pump or piston machine, each shot or serving of espresso should dribble out in about 15 to 20 seconds from the moment the first drop appears. However, gauge when to cut off the flow of coffee by sight, not by clock or timer. The fineness of the grind may vary, as will the pressure you apply when tamping. Consequently, the speed with which the hot water dribbles through the coffee will also vary from serving to serving. If in doubt, cut off the flow of coffee sooner rather than later. Better to experience a perfectly flavored small drink than an obnoxiously bitter large one. As you gauge the flow of coffee keep in mind that it will continue to run into the cup or receptacle for a moment or two after you have turned off the pump or shut off the coffee valve.

If you use a pump or piston machine, brewing into a jigger, or bartender's shot glass, is a simple way of making certain that you do not produce overlong, bitter-tasting shots when you are brewing for frothed-milk drinks. For a classic 1¼-ounce serving, brew the shot, including crema, up to the line on the glass.

If you brewer does *not* have a mechanism for cutting off the flow of the coffee, you will need to improvise. If the design of the machine permits, use two separate coffee-collecting receptacles, one to catch the first rich dribbles, which you will drink, and a second to catch the pale remainder, which you will throw away. Whatever you do, don't spoil the first bloom of coffee by mixing it with the pale, bitter dregs.

Knock-out and Cleaning. Pump and piston machines can be recharged with further doses of coffee while the machines are still hot. To remove spent grounds from a hot filter, turn the filter holder upside down and rap it smartly against the side of a sturdy waste container or against the crosspiece of the waste drawer that may have come with your system. This can be one of those pleasantly nonchalant gestures that perfects itself with time and practice. Aficionados may wish to professionalize by purchasing a small knock-out box of the kind used in small caffès. Wipe any leftover grounds off the edge of the filter holder and fill with the next dose of ground coffee. If significant amounts of spent coffee stick inside the filter you may need to rinse it before refilling.

A few machines may not incorporate a catch to retain the filter inside the holder. In this case you have no recourse, but to dig the grounds out with a spoon.

Regularly wipe off the gasket and shower head on the underside of the group. Spent coffee grains tend to cling there. Less often, pop the filter basket out of the filter holder, and wash both parts. Take note of the manufacturer's instructions for decalcification. If you live in an area with particularly hard water, I would recommend using bottled water, particularly if you own a pump machine. The workings of these machines are especially vulnerable to calcium build-up.

ESPRESSO BREAK
THE CREMA QUESTION

Crema, the natural golden froth that graces the surface of a well-made tazzina of straight espresso, is an almost mystical obsession among Italian espresso lovers. Its only practical role is to help hold in some of the aroma until the coffee is drunk, but its cultural connotations are legion.

For Italian espresso professionals it is the key to diagnosing the coffee underneath. Dark-colored crema indicates a blend heavy with robusta coffees. Golden-colored crema reveals a blend based on higher-quality arabica coffees. Crema made up of a few, large bubbles indicates a coffee that has been brewed too quickly and is probably thin-bodied. Dense, clotted cream indicates a coffee that has been brewed too slowly and may be burned.

For the Italian bar operator crema is the mark of achievement: a perfect golden stream of froth descending majestically from the filter holder is a demonstration, endlessly repeated, of his mastery. For those Italians who simply like good espresso, cream is a visual prelude to the sensual pleasure of the coffee itself, promising sweetness rather than bitterness, rounded richness, rather than one-dimensional thinness.

Perhaps crema suggests even more. A tazzina of espresso without crema stares up with dark, disconcerting blankness, empty of promise, whereas a crema-covered cup seems veiled with intrigue and mystery. Crema intimates grace and elegance, abundance. By comparison a cremaless cup appears exposed and impoverished.

Crema and You

No doubt that last paragraph projects too much, but it is almost impossible to underestimate the role of crema in the mystique of straight espresso. The problem is, a cup of espresso *can* taste just as good without crema as with, and home espresso lovers may find themselves so intimidated by the quest for crema that they may deny themselves the pleasure of enjoying an otherwise good tazzina of cremaless espresso.

So, above all, if your espresso tastes good but has little crema, enjoy the coffee first and worry about how it looks later.

Given that advice, here are a few steps to take if you continue to be concerned about cremaless espresso.

Resign Yourself if You Are Using a Steam-Pressure-Only Brewer.
If you are using a brewer that makes use of the pressure of trapped steam alone to press the brewing water through the coffee (categories 1 and 2, pages 106–7), either give up on crema or buy a pump machine. Because, even if you follow the instructions for brewing on pages 141–

45 very carefully, you will generate only a little crema. Steam-pressure-only brewers will produce reasonably good espresso drinks with milk, but will not produce a straight espresso with the richness and body, *or* the crema, of the caffè product.

Good Technique.
If you are using a pump or piston machine (categories 3 and 4, pages 107–12), begin your pursuit of crema by reviewing your brewing technique against the instructions on page 141–45. Make certain your grind is a fine grit, that you use sufficient coffee, that the coffee is evenly distributed in the filter, and that it has been tamped hard, with a twisting motion of the tamper, to polish the surface of the dose.

Precision Grind.
Above all, review the grind of your coffee. It should be a very fine grit, but also a uniform grit, produced either by a large, commercial grinder in a store, or by a specialized home espresso grinder. See Chapter 7 for more on precision grind and how to get it.

Fresh Coffee.
Make certain your coffee is fresh. If you buy whole bean coffee in bulk, buy it from a vendor who emphasizes freshness, keep it in a sealed container in a cool, dry place, and grind it as close to the moment of brewing as possible. If you use pre-ground, canned coffee, immediately transfer the excess coffee to a sealed container for storage.

Lots of Ground Coffee.
This may qualify as cheating, but often the only way to achieve good crema on some pump ma-

chines is by using more than the recommended amount of coffee per serving. The normal recommended dose of ground coffee per shot of espresso is slightly less than 2 level tablespoons. For better crema use the double filter basket rather than the single and use at least half again as much coffee per serving, or about 3 level tablespoons.

Small, Pre-Warmed Cup. Brew directly into a narrow-sided, 3-ounce demitasse cup that has been pre-warmed. The warm, narrow cup will help build up and hold the crema.

Special Devices to Promote Crema. Some pump machines have special gadgets built into the filter holder to promote the formation of crema. All of those that I've tried help considerably. Unfortunately, you must buy the entire machine to get the gadget, so this solution is only appropriate for those so infatuated by crema that they are willing to purchase a new machine to get it.

Turn Buddhist. Decide that plainness and substance are more important than a little illusory froth.

ESPRESSO BREAK
FROTHING THE MILK

Most Americans prefer their espresso blended with hot, frothed milk. Fortunately, the majority of espresso-brewing appliances now sold in the United States have built-in steam apparatus suitable for frothing milk. If you like espresso drinks with milk, make certain that any espresso brewing device you purchase has such a mechanism.

If the clerk doesn't know what you're talking about, look for a small pipe, usually about ¼ inch in diameter and a few inches long, protruding from the side or front of the device. Some beginner-friendly machines may replace the conventional wand with an automatic milk frother (it looks like a small plastic cylinder protruding from the front of the ma-

chine) that sucks cold milk into one end and squirts out hot frothed milk at the other. These devices may sound wonderful, but in fact are fussy, demanding, and delicate. I would recommend against buying any machine that does not give you the option of replacing the automatic frother with a conventional steam wand.

Heating the milk with the steam wand is easy; producing a head of froth or foam is a little trickier, but like riding a bicycle or centering clay on a potter's wheel, exquisitely simple once you've broken through and gotten the hang of it.

Another alternative for milk frothing is one of the little cylindrical stand-alone devices that look like French-press coffee makers. However, assuming you already have steam up for espresso brewing, it hardly seems worthwhile putting yourself through several additional steps to froth milk when you can do it in thirty seconds using the steam wand on your brewer.

At any rate, the instructions that follow assume you are faced with using a conventional steam wand on a conventional espresso maker. Advice for using the stand-alone frothers appears at the end of this section.

Steps in Making Drinks with Frothed Milk. There are three stages to making an espresso drink with frothead milk. The first is brewing the coffee; the second is frothing and heating the milk; the third is combining the two. Never froth the coffee and milk together, which would stale the fresh coffee and ruin the often eye-pleasing contrast between white

foam and dark coffee. Nor is it a good idea, even if your machine permits it, to simultaneously brew espresso and froth the milk. Concentrate on the brewing operation first, taking care to produce only as much coffee as you need. Then stop the brewing and turn to the frothing operation.

The Frothing Apparatus: The steam wand, also called *steam stylus*, *pipe*, or *nozzle*, is a little tube that protrudes from the top or side of the machine (A). At the tip of the wand are one to four little holes that project jets of steam downward or diagonally when the steam function is activated, or in some cases a special nozzle designed to facilitate the frothing operation. Nearby you will find the knob that controls the flow of steam (B). While you are brewing coffee, this knob and the valve it controls are kept screwed shut.

Some machines do not have a screw knob to control the flow of steam for frothing. Instead, you simply activate the steam function with a switch, automatically releasing what the manufacturer considers to be the optimum flow of steam for the frothing operation.

Still other machines come with aerating nozzles on the end of the steam wand designed to make the frothing operation easier. These devices suck additional room temperature air into the milk along with the steam, presumably helping to fluff up the milk. Most still require a conventional frothing technique as described below, however. They do not replace the traditional frothing procedure; they simply make it easier. However, one aerating nozzle, the Krups Perfect Froth, requires a completely different technique, which is described in

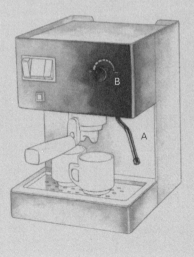

the Krups literature. With virtually any other kind of steam nozzle or apparatus you will find the following instructions helpful, if not essential.

Do not feel deprived if your machine has a conventional or only mildly modified frothing apparatus, by the way. Anyone with the smallest amount of patience can master the normal frothing operation, and in the process gain considerably more control over the texture and dimension of the froth than is possible with the less conventional apparatus. And frothing milk the old-fashioned way may turn out to be one of those noble, Zen-like rituals that stubbornly resist progress, like manual shifting in sports cars, wooden bats in baseball, and catching fish with dry flies.

Frothing Pitchers and Milk Thermometers. Milk can be frothed in any relatively wide-mouthed container that fits under the steam wand of your machine. If you take your drink in a mug, for example, you can simply froth the milk in the same mug you use to consume your drink. However, small stainless steel pitchers designed specifically for milk frothing are useful. They are light in weight, and usually have a broad, rolled pouring lip, which facilitates moving the froth and milk together in one smooth motion from pitcher to cup.

Frothed-milk thermometers resemble meat thermometers, and clip on the edge of the frothing pitcher, with the dial facing up and the temperature probe extending down into the pitcher. These thermometers assist in monitoring the exact heat of the milk under the froth (135°F. if you plan to enjoy your drink immediately, up to 165° if there will be a delay in

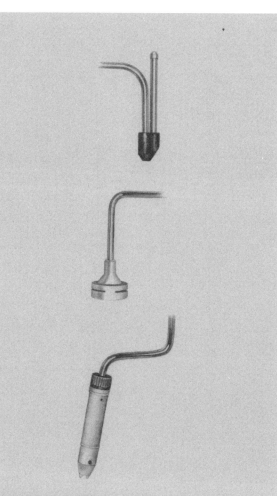

Three aerating nozzles designed to make milk-frothing easier. The removable Krups Perfect Froth device, top; *the Braun Turbo Cappuccino, which incorporates a little spinning, fan-like element inside the nozzle,* center; *and the Saeco Cappuccino,* bottom. *The majority of espresso brewing devices sold in North America now incorporate such nozzles.*

serving or drinking it), and help the novice avoid one of the most prevalent errors of milk frothing: overheating or scalding the milk. However, I find that simply feeling the bottom of the milk frothing container (when it's too hot to touch, stop frothing) works just as well.

The Milk. Virtually any liquid dairy product, from skim milk to heavy cream, plus most imitation liquid dairy products such as soy milk, can be frothed using the steam apparatus of an espresso brewing device. More on choosing milk for espresso drinks is given in Chapter 9. Milk with more butterfat maybe slightly easier to froth for beginners than milk with less.

Transition between Brewing and Frothing. In less expensive, steam-pressure machines (category 2, pages 106–7), and in piston machines (category 4, pages 111–12) this transition is accomplished simply by closing the coffee-brewing valve or ending the coffee-brewing operation and opening the steam valve. In button-operated pump machines (category 4, pages 111–12), there is usually a more complex transitional procedure, which will be described in the instructions accompanying your machine. The transition involves raising the temperature of the boiler where the water is heated from the somewhat lower temperature best for brewing to a higher temperature suitable for producing steam. You press a button or trigger a switch and wait twenty or thirty seconds for the boiler to achieve the higher temperature. In such machines it is *particularly important to bleed the hot water from the steam pipe before beginning to froth milk,* since a sub-

stantial residue of water usually collects in the pipe during brewing, which can dilute the milk. Place an empty frothing pitcher or cup under the steam wand and open the valve. Wait until all of the hot water has sputtered out of pipe and a steady hiss of steam is escaping the nozzle before beginning the frothing operation.

A Dry Run. Before attempting to froth milk for the first time, practice opening and closing the steam valve with the machine on, the brewing function off or closed, and the steam function activated. Get a general sense of how many turns it takes to create a explosive jet of steam, and how many to permit a steady, powerful jet. It is the latter intensity that you will use to froth milk: not so powerful that the jet produces an overpowering roar, but powerful enough to produce a strong, steady hiss.

Note that steam cools rapidly as it exits the nozzle of the wand. Even four inches from the nozzle the steam is merely wet to the touch (try it) and presents no danger of injury. Hot milk churning or spattering out of the pitcher during incorrect frothing can cause mild burns, however. Follow the instructions below carefully.

The Frothing Routine
- Fill the container or cup *no more than halfway* with cold milk (the colder the better; hot milk will not produce froth).
- Open the steam valve for a few seconds to bleed any hot water from inside the wand into an empty cup or container. Then close the valve until just a tiny bit of steam is escap-

ing from the tip of the wand. This is to prevent milk from being sucked back up into the wand as you immerse it into the milk.

- Holding the container vertically, immerse the tip of the wand deeply into the milk (A). Slowly open the valve, then gradually close it until you get a strong, but not explosive, release of steam that moves the surface of the milk, but doesn't wildly churn it.

- Now slowly lower the milk container, thus bringing the tip of the wand closer to the surface of the milk (B). When the wand tip is just below the surface of the milk you will hear a rough-edged hissing sound, the surface will begin to seethe, and frothy bubbles will begin to form. If the wand tip is too deep in the milk, there will be no hiss and the surface will not seethe; if it is too shallow, milk will spatter onto the sides of the pitcher (and possibly onto your hand and apron). If it is just right, a gratifying head of froth will begin to rise from the surface of the milk. You need to follow the froth upward as it develops. Listen for the hiss; if you don't hear it, or if it turns to a dull rumble, the wand is too deep in the milk.

- The first swelling of froth will be made up of largish, unstable bubbles. Periodically drop the tip of the steam wand back into the milk and hold it there for a moment, to let some of these bubbles pop and settle. Then bring the tip of the wand back to just below the surface of the milk again to rebuild the head of froth. Repeat this process until you have a creamy, dense head of froth made up of a stable matrix of tiny bubbles.

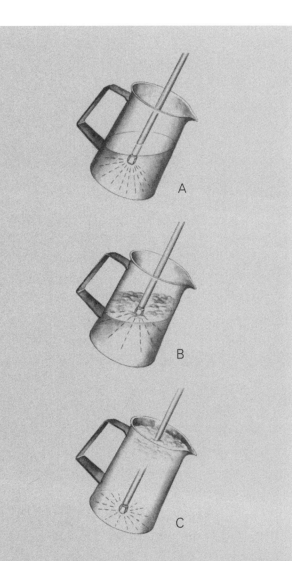

Heating the Milk. At this point, feel the sides of the milk container to determine whether the milk is hot. If not, lower the wand tip completely into the milk and keep it there until the container's sides are just a little too hot to be touched comfortably (C). See pages 149–50 if you are using a milk thermometer.

Never heat the milk to boiling, and again, always froth the milk first, before you heat it, since cold milk froths best. If you are frothing milk for the first time and you end up with hot milk and not much froth, enjoy what you have and try again later with cold milk.

Finishing the Frothing Operation. Always conclude by opening the steam valve for a few seconds to clear milk residues from the nozzle. If you are using an inexpensive machine that utilizes simple steam pressure to force the water through the coffee, it is a good idea to let the steam valve remain open after you turn off the machine, to bleed the remaining steam from the boiler and relieve pressure on the valves and gaskets. The simpler steam apparatus only require wiping with a damp cloth; some of the more complex aerating frothing nozzles need to be periodically dissembled and the parts thoroughly cleaned.

Occasionally milk residues may completely clog the tiny holes through which the steam issues, in which case you will need to poke them open with a needle. Perform this operation with the steam valve *closed,* to avoid a sudden blast of hot steam.

If you don't immediately raise an impressive head of froth, be patient. You may have to suffer through a few naked cappuccini at first, but inside a week you'll be frothing like a Milanese master.

Other Uses for the Steam Function. The steam wand also can be used to heat hot chocolate concentrate for various espresso-chocolate drinks (see pages 130–31), and to preheat cups and glasses by bathing their insides with steam. In most pump machines the steam wand also will deliver hot water for tea and other beverages; see the instructions that come with your machine.

Using a French Press–Style Milk Frother. These stand-alone devices are beginner friendly and produce a heavy but satisfactory froth. You put milk in a metal or glass cylinder and pump the frothing head through it until it achieves the texture you require. Unfortunately, heating the milk is a separate (and clumsy) operation. With some designs you are advised to put the metal-free cylinder with its charge of milk in the microwave. With others you need to heat the milk on the stove. The two-step procedure rapidly becomes annoying. If you brew espresso I recommend you learn to froth milk using the steam wand. It's quicker, simpler, and, again, not that difficult.

ESPRESSO BREAK

TROUBLE-SHOOTING FOR BREWING AND FROTHING

Coffee Brewing

Machine is on, but no coffee appears.

- Coffee valve is not open, or brewing switch is not on.
- Steam valve is open and pressure is escaping out of steam wand.
- There is no water in boiler (for steam pressure and piston machines) or in reservoir (for pump machines). In pump machines, the removable reservoir may not be properly seated.
- Coffee is too finely ground, too powdery, or tamped too firmly. If coffee valve is open, or brewing switch on and boiler or reservoir is full, and still no coffee appears, *immediately turn off power or heat,* wait until device cools, and reload with a somewhat coarser grind of coffee, tamped less firmly.
- Pump or other inner workings may be clogged with calcium deposits. Decalcify according to manufacturer's directions.

Coffee gushes out; tastes thin and bitter.

- Coffee grind is not fine enough; coffee has not been evenly distributed and tamped firmly in filter.
- Not enough coffee in filter.

Coffee oozes out slowly; tastes burned or baked.

- Coffee has been ground too finely, and/or tamped too firmly. Coarsen grind, ease up on tamping, or use less coffee.

Coffee appears very watery; looks and tastes thin.

- Water may be escaping around edges of filter holder and dripping directly into cup without passing through coffee. Make certain filter holder is firmly and evenly snugged in place; make certain lumps of coffee grains have not interfered with seal around edges of filter holder. If machine is old, gasket on underside of group may be worn or compressed permitting leakage. Check gasket and replace if necessary.

Coffee dribbles out properly, but still tastes thin and bitter.

- Brew coffee according to instructions on pages 141–45. Do not allow excessive water to run through ground coffee. Brew only 1 to 1½ ounces espresso per serving or dose of ground coffee.
- With a pump machine, make certain that you move the receptacle containing brewed coffee out from under filter holder and group while you froth milk. Pump machines tend to drip during the frothing operation, sometimes diluting an otherwise well-brewed serving of espresso.

Straight espresso tastes good, but lacks crema.

- With steam-pressure machines: Significant crema is almost impossible to achieve with steam-pressure brewers. Occasionally some can be gotten by using large doses of

153

fresh coffee and by following brewing instructions on pages 141–45 meticulously.

- With pump or piston machines: Use fresh coffee; use plenty of it; make certain coffee is ground with precision on a large commercial grinder or a specialized home espresso grinder (see Chapter 7); tamp coffee firmly with twisting motion of tamper to polish surface of coffee; brew into a pre-heated, half-size cup (tazzina, demitasse) to compress and exaggerate crema. For more on crema production, see pages 145–47.

Coffee has good flavor, but is thin and lacks body.

- With steam-pressure machines: Follow instructions for good espresso brewing, pages 141–45. Even at best, espresso brewed with steam-pressure machines will not be as rich and full-bodied as espresso produced by pump and piston machines.
- With pump or piston machines: Follow instructions for good espresso brewing, pages 141–45, with particular attention to fine, precise grind.
- Increase amount of ground coffee per serving.

Colffee has good body and richness, but tastes too sharp.

- Coffee is probably too darkly roasted or too acidy for your taste. Choose a coffee blended and roasted for northern Italian taste. In a specialty store ask the clerk for a sweet, mild blend; in a pre-ground, canned espresso coffee look for one roasted and blended in Italy; in a straight, un-blended coffee try dark-roast Mexico Coatepac or Oaxaca, Peru, or Brazil Bourbon Santos.

Coffee has good body, but tastes too bland. Flavor of coffee dies out in frothed-milk drinks.

- Coffee is probably too lightly roasted or too mild for your taste. Choose a coffee somewhat darker in roast, with an oily surface, blended for West Coast American taste. In a pre-ground, canned coffee try a coffee roasted and blended for Latin taste; in a straight, unblended coffee, try dark-roast Kenya, Yemen, Colombia, or Guatemala.

Coffee tastes good but straight shots are lukewarm.

- Pre-heat group, filter holder, and filter by running hot brewing water though them before beginning brewing operation. Brew directly into a pre-heated cup.

Milk Frothing

Frothing valve is open, but no steam comes out of nozzle.

- Steam valve is not open, or not opened sufficiently.
- Nozzle openings may be clogged with milk residue. Close steam valve, turn off and cool down machine, and thoroughly clean nozzle, opening clogged holes with a needle.
- Boiler or water reservoir may be empty; in pump machines removable water reservoir may not be properly seated.

Steam issuing from nozzle is weak, even with valve fully open.

- In a pump machine:

    Make certain stream function is activated and ready light is on.

    If you have frothed milk for more than one drink, you may have temporarily exhausted steam supply in boiler. Wait until ready light goes on again, then resume frothing.

- Clean nozzle and nozzle outlets.

After frothing, milk tastes weak and diluted.

- In a pump machine, make certain all hot water has been bled from steam pipe beginning to froth. See page 150.

After following all frothing directions on pages 147–52, you still can't get milk to froth.

- Start with cold milk, not warm or hot. Froth milk first, then heat it. When frothing, make certain nozzle head is just below surface of milk, producing a bubbly, rough-edged hiss, and causing surface of milk to seethe.
- Relax. It will come.

Espresso-and-frothed milk drinks taste watery and lack richness.

- Use whole milk rather than milk with reduced butterfat.
- Brew coffee according to instructions on pages 141–45. Do not allow excessive water to run through ground coffee. Brew only 1 to 1½ ounces espresso per serving of ground coffee.
- Increase the amount of ground coffee per serving.

10 CARTS, CAFFÈS, AND HOUSES

ESPRESSO PLACES

Some years ago I was sitting in downtown Seattle over an empty cappuccino cup near one of Seattle's ubiquitous espresso carts. This particular cart was nestled under the marquee of the Coliseum Theater, a landmark movie palace from the early days of cinema then closed and waiting for someone with money to turn it into boutiques. The cart was owned by Chuck Beek, one of the entrepreneurs credited with starting Seattle's historic espresso cart business.

I assume most readers now are familiar with espresso carts: espresso bars on wheels, complete with machine, grinder, small refrigerator, and the rest of the gear needed to produce espresso cuisine, all neatly built into a cart compact enough for one or two people to roll out of seclusion every morning into some promising urban setting filled with passing potential espresso buyers. An innovator named Craig Donarum built Seattle's first espresso cart in 1980, sold that cart to Chuck Beek some months later, and from that one cart hundreds more have sprung, to the point that hardly a large filling station or supermarket in the Seattle area doesn't have an espresso cart or stand in front of it, dispensing Italian coffees to passing shoppers and motorists.

Chuck's newest cart under the Coliseum Theater marquee was surrounded by a few tables and chairs, some T-shirts and postcards, and a neon sign, which read simply CAFFEINE. On that morning there were three or four people lined up at the cart buying caffè lattes to take back to work, some of them exchanging neighborhood and workplace gossip with Chuck. The tables were occupied by people doing the time-honored things people do while drinking coffee: one

man was reading a newspaper, several well-dressed women were holding an animated conversation (I later learned they worked at the nearby Nordstrom department store), and I was sitting as I have for so many hours of my life, looking at the world from over my recently emptied cappuccino cup and thinking.

FROM CAIRO TO COFFEE CART

My thoughts on that morning had taken off from espresso carts and landed, after some detours, several centuries back at coffee's first breakout into the streets, when entrepreneurs took coffee beyond the confines of Muslim Sufi meetings in early sixteenth-century Cairo and created history's first ad hoc coffeehouses. These informal, open-air establishments were probably more coffee stands or kiosks than houses, and must in many ways have resembled Chuck Beek's cart in Seattle. The illustrations that accompany nineteenth-century European travelers' accounts give the impression, for example, that the less formal coffeehouses of Muslim tradition were simple, open-air pavilions or kiosks that, like Chuck Beek's operation, simply slipped into unused urban spaces and allowed their seating arrangements to spill casually out into the streets. The customers sitting at the tables in these illustrations look to be occupying themselves in much the same way as those of us sitting under the Coliseum Theater marquee in 1992: some quietly talking, others alone, lost in thought, observing the passing scene, or reading, but all representing aspects of the peculiar sort of semi-intellectual loafing—reading, talking, writing, playing chess, staring into space, and

thinking—typical of coffeehouses, cafés, and caffès throughout history.

Resistance to Improvised Institutions

It is even possible to see a parallel between the resistance these early coffeehouses suffered from religious and secular authorities and the (albeit much milder) resistance the Seattle espresso carts faced fifteen or twenty years ago, when they were hounded by municipal authorities for lacking proper equipment and permits. In both cases rather humble urban entrepreneurs and their coffee-drinking clientele managed in the end to triumph over the resistance of authorities to the irregularities presented by such improvised institutions. And in both cases we can sense the liveliness and humanity such operations bring to the urban scene, the way the simple presence of a cart selling coffee and a few tables and chairs can transform a corner that (in the case of Chuck Beek's operation) otherwise would have been deserted, inhabited only by scraps of newspaper and weeds poking out of the sidewalk. An espresso machine and a few tables and chairs instantly create a place where you can *be* rather than simply pass through.

There is an even more humble archetype of public coffee selling that has an equally long history: the coffee vendor, the lone man (or woman) with a pot of coffee, a few cups, and a stool, who wanders the streets and sets up wherever somebody slows down long enough to drink a cup of coffee. References to such entrepreneurs abound in the published history of coffee. An eighteenth-century illustration of a Near Eastern coffee vendor is reproduced on page 161. I hardly expected to encounter similar shoestring entrepreneurs in the 1990s, but given the popularity of espresso drinks, I should have known better. While waiting in a cab in a toll line in Boston a few years ago, I saw a robust young man striding between the stopped cars, a sort of insulated tank on his back, a cup dispenser on his belt, and a sign advertising CAFFÈ LATTE on his chest, serving hot coffee and consolation through car windows to frustrated motorists.

Design vs. Serendipity

The capacity for a modest, self-contained espresso-selling operation to transform a dead space that people simply walk through on their way to somewhere else into a lively arena for human interaction and contemplation has, of course, not gone unnoticed by planners, architects, and building owners. Just across the street from Chuck Beek's espresso cart was a Starbucks espresso kiosk, situated in the glossy lobby of the City Centre building.

Although the Starbucks organization started as a small coffee chain and continues to exhibit an impressive passion for quality, it nevertheless is an operation for the most part antithetical to Chuck Beek's: enormous in scale, sleek if not slick in its handling of marketing, graphics, and architecture, partnered with a quantity of other corporate gorillas, and traded on stock exchanges. That contrast in style and scale was displayed here: the Starbucks kiosk was splendidly designed and exquisitely situated among indoor plants and marble, the result of careful design rather than casual serendipity like Chuck's location across the street. Nevertheless, the continuity with the first coffeehouses and kiosks in sixteenth-century Cairo continues to be striking: again a public space, in this case impressive but impersonal, filled with benches that only an architect could love, is transformed into a space where people, at least briefly, talk, read, and contemplate over coffee. Even the open, pavilionlike

Throughout its history coffee has been sold by strolling street vendors, who in effect bring the coffeehouse to the customer. This vendor, as depicted in an early eighteenth-century French travel book, looks obviously undercapitalized but is nevertheless elegant in gesture and clearly confident of his product.

161

design of the Starbucks installation suggests the continuity with the very beginnings of the public celebration of coffee.

A PECULIAR STYLE OF MENTAL RECREATION

It remains an open question whether the particular brand of intellectual loafing associated with the coffeehouse from its inception: reading, talking, chess playing, and staring into space and thinking, is directly related to the special kind of mental intoxication peculiar to coffee and caffeine (I believe that it is), or whether the character of the coffeehouse, once established, simply maintained itself for other cultural reasons. What is certain is that as coffee spread through the world so did the coffeehouse and its peculiar style of mental recreation. From Cairo it was carried to Syria, from Syria to Turkish Constantinople, from Turkey to Venice via trade, and to Vienna via the failed Turkish siege of that city in 1683. From Venice and Vienna the habit of coffee and coffeehouses spread to the rest of Western Europe, and from there to North America.

ESPRESSO REDEFINES THE AMERICAN COFFEE PLACE

The first American coffeehouses were modeled on those in England, but appear to have been more taverns and inns than coffeehouses in either the Muslim or the modern sense. How these early tavern-coffeehouses evolved into the array of coffee-drinking establishments familiar to North Americans of the 1950s (the coffee shop of vinyl booths and bottomless cup, the diner, the roadside café and truck stop) is not clear. But what is clear is that espresso, arriving from Italy in the 1930s through 1950s, has redefined the North American coffeehouse and café.

Espresso from its inception was a public phenomenon, the application of technology to coffee making on a scale difficult to duplicate at home, at least until recently. It permitted the production of a coffee so technically superior to the simpler coffees Italians brewed at home that it added a technical reason to the social reasons for taking coffee in public. Not only was it more fun to drink coffee in a bar of caffè, but with the advent of espresso the coffee tasted better than coffee brewed at home, and embodied a mystique or glamour as well.

From Club to Caffè

Espresso appears to have been introduced into American life by Italian immigrants, who established informal social clubs, places where men from the Italian-American community met to drink coffee from the recently popularized espresso machines, play cards, talk, and cut business deals. The transformation of these social clubs into public caffès, where the Italians were joined and often displaced by the writ-

Coffeehouses along a river in Damascus, as depicted in an early nineteenth-century engraving. The informality of the arrangements in these places mirrors a similar informality in today's impromptu street cafés created by espresso carts and stands.

ers, artists, and intellectuals who found a sympathetic atmosphere in Italian-American neighborhoods, was a gradual development, and one that in some places still continues.

One of the most fashionable places to take a cappuccino in San Francisco during the late 1980s, for example, was a small, plain Italian cigar-store-cum-caffè, which, like so many similar places before it, was in the process of changing from neighborhood

hangout for local Italians to destination for in-the-know artists, writers, and professionals. On the other, earlier end of the chronology, the first American espresso caffè for which I have a date is Caffè Reggio in New York's Greenwich Village. The Caffè Reggio was founded as a social club in 1927, but by the 1950s had been pretty much converted to an artists' and writers' hangout. It is still in business, by the way. The original espresso machine has been retired to icon status in one corner, but the 1930s Little Italy, garage-sale baroque furniture and bric-a-brac interior continues splendidly intact.

Espresso Goes to College

By the 1950s Italian-Americans were opening caffès that, from their inception, catered to a mix of patrons, including both Italian-Americans and a local mélange of writers, artists, and similar types. Many of these postwar establishments were situated in university communities, like the Caffè Mediterraneum in Berkeley (opened in 1958). I clearly recall the mid-1960s crowd in the Mediterraneum, which typically combined students; a few faculty; some older intellectuals whose main function in life seemed to be sitting at the same table every day and pontificating to one another; various brands of radicals, from early Black Power advocates to orthodox Marxists to sentimental Trotskyists; and a table of Italian locals from the neighborhood, including the mailman and the barber from next door.

Today college communities continue to support a growing espresso caffè culture, as American students discover what their French counterparts have known for centuries: that studying at a marble-top table over a cappuccino (or café crème beats the library every time. The commitment of student communities to espresso often can be fierce and rather exclusive. A friend reports walking into a large caffè opposite the University of California at Berkeley and asking for coffee. "We don't serve *coffee*," growled the barman in response. "We only serve *espresso*."

MUSIC AND SUBVERSION

Patrons at early Middle Eastern coffeehouses didn't restrict themselves to reading, talking, and contemplating. They also listened to music, watched puppet shows, and listened to storytellers and other performers. "Generally in the coffeehouses there are many violins, flute players, and musicians, who are hired by the proprietor of the coffeehouse to play and sing much of the day, with the end of drawing in customers," wrote Jean de Thevenot in his seventeenth-century account of Turkish coffeehouses.

There was also considerable concern among political authorities regarding the nature of the talk that went on at sixteenth- and seventeenth-century coffeehouses, both in the Near East and in Europe. With so many people spending so many hours comparing notes on the events of the day, might not the conclusions they reached be dangerous to the current political and social order? This fear more than any other probably lay behind the numerous early efforts to suppress coffeehouses. Charles II of England, for example, in his very short-lived (eleven day!) suppression of coffeehouses in 1675, contended that "in such houses . . . divers false, malitious and scandalous reports are devised and spread abroad to the Defamation of His Majestie's Government, and to the Disturbance of the Peace and Quiet of the Realm."

Monarchical Misgivings

Events in the eighteenth century seemed to confirm such monarchical misgivings. Coffee and coffeehouses are credited with roles in both the French and

American revolutions, as well as in the Enlightenment, the period in Western thought that planted the seeds of those revolutions. The famous Parisian Café Procope was the regular haunt of Enlightenment thinkers like Voltaire and Condorcet, and Camille Desmoulins' speech at the Café Foy is said to have set off the first overtly rebellious act of the French Revolution, the storming of the Bastille. Across the Atlantic, Boston's famous coffeehouse, the Green Dragon, was called, in an often-cited description by Daniel Webster, "the headquarters of the Revolution."

ANOTHER ARCHETYPE

Such potentially subversive carrying on, combined with the long-established coffeehouse custom of offering small-scale, informal entertainment, connects most clearly with still another North American archetype of the public dispensing of espresso, the counterculture coffeehouse, the candle-in-a-bottle, poster-on-the-wall, informal nightclub of the rebels, poets, Beats, and folk and jazz lovers of the 1950s. Such places, which in the 1950s often appeared in the same neighborhoods as the Italian-American social clubs turned espresso caffès noted earlier, were usually opened by artist-musician-writer types to cater to the same, and put less emphasis on espresso, reading, and contemplation than their Italian-American counterparts, and a bit more on music, performance, wine, and beer.

The counterculture coffeehouse appeared on its way out during the sleek 1980s, but it has now made a robust comeback in urban pockets all over the country, from Los Angeles to Seattle, where if I had risen from my table under the Coliseum Theater marquee that day in the early 1990s and walked south a few blocks, I could have taken an excellent espresso at a dozen classic coffeehouses, where by day a sleepy restfulness prevails, while you feel the casual artist funk of the decor waiting for nightfall and the arrival of the first musicians and performers.

Intimacy and Experiment

Coffeehouses provided and still provide a range of cultural possibility that is virtually unique in our society: they function as the usual coffee-culture hangouts for reading, talking, and contemplation; as art galleries free of the taste-making controls of commercial galleries; as informal nightclubs free of the taste-making controls of the commercial music industry; and as places where artists and performers as diverse as poets, stand-up comedians, magicians, political satirists, and belly dancers can entertain their own small but passionate audiences, nurturing an aesthetic culture based on face-to-face intimacy and experiment rather than passive consumption of media and spectacle.

It is difficult to determine how important espresso in particular, and coffee generally, are to the gestalt of the counterculture coffeehouse, since beer and wine are usually also consumed there. But the historical association of coffeehouses with a sort of alternative aesthetic culture suggests that the particular mental intoxication of caffeine and coffee, a sort of individualistic mental reverie, promotes a different kind of cultural stance, and a different kind of art, than the

London youths stimulate themselves at one of the some 2,000 espresso bars that dotted Great Britain during the British espresso bar craze of the post-World-War-II period. No doubt a Vespa or Lambretta waited just outside the door. By the 1970s it was hard to find an espresso in Great Britain, though a revival is now underway.

THE SPECIALTY COFFEE CONTRIBUTION

The last strand of recent coffee history to contribute to contemporary espresso culture is what is often called specialty coffee, a phenomenon that, like the Italian-American caffè and the counterculture coffeehouse, was born (or reborn) in the 1950s and has been gaining momentum ever since. The specialty coffee store is, of course, the place where you buy, usually in bulk, coffees with names like Ethiopian Harrar or Sumatran Lintong, or (if the store owner is not a purist) Chocolate Mint or Irish Creme. These stores are based on the nineteenth- and early twentieth-century tradition of small stores that roasted their own coffee in a little machine behind the counter and sold it directly to the public in bulk, custom ground. A few specialty stores are direct survivors from that period, but most are the brain children of pioneering entrepreneurs who recreated the tradition with skill and passion. As the quality of mass-distributed, canned coffee declined in the 1960s and 1970s owing to the substitution of bland, cheap robusta coffee for higher-quality arabica coffees, the specialty coffee business picked up steam, first in university towns and gentrified urban pockets, then in city centers and suburban malls. From a few coffee-loving idealists scratching a living from behind pine counters, the specialty coffee world has grown to become a powerful alternative to the commercial coffee business, with a specialty coffee trade association, publications, meetings, industry giants like Starbucks, and other trappings of an established niche-occupier in modern commerce.

more diffused, often soggier and more collective euphoria of alcohol. If so, coffee and the espresso machine are central to the maverick contribution that the American coffeehouse has made and continues to make to North American aesthetic culture.

Caffès Despite Themselves

Espresso was not central to the interests of the early pioneers of specialty coffee, who preferred to devote themselves to delicious subtleties like the differences between Ethiopian Harrar and Ethiopian Yirgacheffe, or to the nuances of original house blends. Nevertheless, as specialty coffee stores began to accommodate their customers by adding tables, chairs, and pastries, dispensing espresso also became an important part of their business. The omnipresent Starbucks started as a small chain of classic specialty coffee stores, morphed into a mammoth chain of high-quality espresso bars, and now is intent on opening larger locations that function like genuine community coffee houses.

Even specialty stores that once did their best to avoid becoming caffè-ified, like the California-based Peet's chain, were turned by their admirers, willy-nilly, into improvised caffès. I recall driving through North Berkeley, seeing a crowd ahead of me, and thinking that perhaps a serious accident had occurred because so many people were milling around at the edge of the street. Then I realized that they were all holding coffee cups, and that I simply had happened upon the morning crowd at the original Vine Street Peet's store. Such, once more, is the civilizing function of coffee—it can turn even a curb and a piece of dirty sidewalk into a place to talk and be.

ESPRESSO BREAK

CAFFEINE, THE DOCTORS, AND ESPRESSO

Even bringing up health in a book on espresso may strike some readers as contradictory. Although coffee first appeared in human culture as a medicine, the kind we now patronize as "herbal," the modern medical establishment has viewed coffee over the years with suspicion. So much so that coffee has become one of the most intensely scrutinized of modern foods and beverages.

Why has the medical establishment chosen to focus so much attention on coffee in particular? Why not on scores of other foods, from white mushrooms to black pepper to spinach, all of which have been accused of promoting various diseases? Perhaps because coffee is such an appealing dietary scapegoat. Since it has no nutritive value and makes us feel good for no reason, coffee may end up higher on the medical hit list than other foods or beverages that may offer equal or greater grounds for suspicion, but are more nourishing and less fun.

And since in its dark, syrupy richness espresso seems an intensification of the very idea of coffee, some readers also may worry that espresso is an intensification of coffee's purported health risks.

For Now, Sip Easy

For now, however, the espresso lover can rest easy, or at least sip easy. Despite over twenty-five years of intensive study, medical science has yet to prove any definite connection between moderate caffeine or coffee consumption and disease or birth defects. For every study that tentatively suggests a relationship between moderate coffee drinking and some disease, or between moderate coffee drinking during pregnancy and a pattern of birth defects, other studies—usually involving larger test populations or more stringent controls—are published that contradict the earlier, critical studies. It is safe to say that the medical profession is further away than ever from nailing coffee with the kind of warning labels that decorate wine and beer bottles, despite continued intensive testing and study.

Nor do espresso drinkers appear to be at any greater risk than their filter-drinking colleagues. Although scientific studies of the impact of coffee on health seldom isolated variables like brewing method and style of roast, nothing in the literature so far would indicate that any characteristic specific to espresso poses special health risks, aside from the fact that it tastes so good we may be tempted to drink too much of it.

In fact, there may even be some basis for arguing that espresso is healthier, or at least less unhealthy, than the ordinary thin-bodied stuff found in restaurant carafes. The darker roasts used in the espresso cuisine contain somewhat less caffeine than lighter roasted coffees, and considerably less of the components that contribute to the acidic sensation that some people blame for their stomach problems. Furthermore, the espresso method extracts somewhat less caffeine from an equivalent amount of ground coffee than does the drip method because the brewing process happens so much faster.

However, such speculation is irresponsible at this point. Until the researchers begin to take the details of brewing method, style of roast, and serving customs (Do the tested subjects take their coffee with milk or without? With sugar or without? Do they tend to drink it on an empty stomach, or after dinner? Do they often take it with alcohol?) into account in their investigations, not only will we know nothing verifiable about the differences between espresso and filter coffee in terms of impact on health, but we probably won't know much about the health impact of coffee generally.

Any Conclusions?

Despite all of the uncertainties, is there anything the health-conscious espresso lover should conclude from the evidence gathered so far? The following, I would argue.

1) If you are a moderate espresso drinker (that is, if you don't regularly indulge in doubles and triples and are capable of waiting a couple of hours between servings), and are in good health, then you should relax and enjoy. Nothing has been proven against temperate coffee or espresso drinking, and for the near future at least, it appears that nothing will be.

"Coffee Comes to the Aid of the Muse," a nineteenth-century painting, illustrates in poetic terms the short-term advantages of coffee for the creative endeavor.

On the other hand:

2) Make certain your espresso drinking *is* moderate. The studies that appear to exonerate coffee drinking are not exonerating the habits of mindless coffeeholics who drink ten cups a day out of the office carafe, or espresso fanatics who pour down triple lattes or double espressos at every coffee break. What is being exonerated is "moderate" intake of caffeine, usually defined as 300 to 500 milligrams per day, or the equivalent of three to five cups of American-style drip coffee (assuming the coffee drinker is not also consuming caffeinated colas or over-the-counter medicines containing caffeine).

Unfortunately, it is not clear how much caffeine a single serving of espresso packs, since espresso brewing procedures differ so widely. A *properly* concentrated, properly pressed 1¼-ounce serving of espresso probably contains about 80 to 100 mg of caffeine, a bit less than the average cup of filter coffee. So, following the definition of moderation in coffee drinking given above, you could consume three to four such proper servings of espresso per day and still remain safely in the "moderate" coffee-drinker category. However, the misplaced generosity of many North American espresso operators place such estimates in question, since these inexperienced zealots tend to continue pressing caffeine and bitter chemicals out of the ground coffee long after the flavor oils had been extracted. If you care about your caffeine intake and love espresso, learn to brew it yourself or patronize places that understand the espresso cuisine and press the coffee properly.

3) If you are pregnant or have certain health conditions, you should bring your coffee-drinking habit to the attention of your physician, even if it is a moderate habit. Aside from pregnancy, health conditions that merit examining your coffee drinking include benign breast lumps, high cholesterol, heart disease, osteoporosis, and some digestive complaints. Again, *nothing has been proven against moderate coffee consumption* in any of these situations, but overall results are ambiguous, some physicians may disagree with certain studies that exonerate caffeine, and new studies may have appeared that complicate the matter.

Finally, and above all:

4) Enjoy rather than swill. In espresso good health and good aesthetics go hand in hand. The Italian practice of stopping frequently during the day to concentrate on the brief but repeated pleasure of a single *small* serving of espresso is probably considerably healthier than the North American practice of carrying off triple lattes or double cappuccinos to work. Espresso drinkers who learn to appreciate the perfection of a single, correctly pressed serving of espresso, or the few fragrant ounces of a classic cappuccino, and who take the time to give themselves over to the experience of that perfection, to the *moment* of the coffee, to its warmth and perfume, are far less likely to abuse caffeine than are those coffee drinkers who carry around plastic foam cups of dead office coffee or half-cold caffè latte all day.

For a discussion of caffeine-free coffees turn to pages 75–78. I discuss caffeine-free coffees and health issues at greater length in my book *Coffee: A Guide to Buying, Brewing, & Enjoying*

SOURCES

Finding Espresso Coffee and Equipment

In an ideal coffee world we would buy our beans a day out of the roaster from the person who had just roasted them, and our equipment at a small specialty store staffed by passionate, knowledgeable clerks ready to provide an endless stream of coffee advice.

In fact, there are coffee stores like that, and they are, without doubt, the best place to buy your coffee and espresso gear. However, we also often are faced with well-meaning but barely informed teenagers staffing chain stores at the end of a half-hour drive on a crowded freeway. In which case, you may be better off buying over the Internet or by catalog. Here is some advice for pursuing both store and Web strategies.

Buying in Person

Coffee. I discuss general retail sources for espresso coffees in Chapter 6. Coffee specialty stores can usually be found in the yellow pages under the "Coffee Dealer, Retail" heading. The qualities to look for in a coffee store are volume and commitment to selling coffee rather than gourmet hams and deli sandwiches. Small, locally based coffee companies that roast right in the store or close by are wonderful. Larger quality-oriented chains like Starbucks, Peet's, Allegro, Timo-

thy's World Coffee, and so on, continue to produce very high-quality coffee despite their size. What should be avoided are places where coffee is an afterthought, a row of dusty bags half-forgotten in a corner.

Equipment. Some categories of espresso equipment are easier to find than others. Caffettiere (Category 1, page 106), small electric steam-pressure countertop brewers (Category 2, pages 106–7), the cheaper pump machines (Category 3, pages 107–111), and general-purpose grinders are now stocked in most upscale department stores, and even carried by some chain discount stores. Most Starbucks stores stock a small but well-selected range of pump espresso machines, matching grinders, and espresso paraphernalia.

Specialized espresso grinders, larger pump and automatic machines, manual piston machines (category 4, pages 111–12), and specialized espresso accessories usually only can be obtained in particularly well-stocked specialty coffee stores or through the mails or internet. Finally, some kinds of equipment—home roasting apparatus, knock-out boxes, and the more exotic piston machines—may be difficult to find in person no matter where you shop. With these unusual apparatus it is probably best to start with the internet.

Buying by Internet or Telephone

Amazingly, at this writing no single Internet site offers the customer a choice of coffees produced by a variety of roasting companies, though one well-established site, *www.coffeereview.com,* does provide authoritative reviews of a wide range of coffees plus links to sites where those coffees can be purchased.

Single-roaster sites are numerous and sell only the coffees of the roasting companies that support these sites. I can mention only a few of the many of interest to espresso aficionados. Torrefazione Italia (*www. titalia.com,* 800-827-2333) specializes in espresso and offers the aficionado a wide range of excellent blends (Perugia for straight espresso and Napoli for milk-heavy drinks have the most fans), although the coffee content on the Torrefazione site is rather fluffy. Other companies do not specialize in espresso but offer a particularly wide range of darker roasted coffees appropriate for espresso brewing. Peet's Coffee & Tea (*www.peets.com,* 800-999-2132) is an especially useful site, since all of Peet's coffees, regardless of name or origin, are dark-roasted and make interesting espresso. Other companies may not dark-roast all of their coffees, but offer a wider range of dark-roasted coffees than is typical. Just three of many are Allegro Coffee (*www.allegro-coffee.com,* 800-666-4869), Armeno Coffee (*www.armeno.com,* 800-276-3661), and Thanksgiving Coffee (*www.thanksgivingcoffee.com,* 800-648-6491). Beware of some roasters that, rather than dark-roasting all of their coffees, simply burn them. The signs of heavy-handed dark roasting are a sharp, thin taste dominated by charred tones and an absence of depth and sweetness.

Mr. Espresso is a family-run roasting company that produces particularly supple, smooth Italian-style espresso coffees on traditional oak-fired roasting machines. At this writing the company has no website; call 510-287-5200 or fax 510-287-5204. Try the Gold Medal Blend.

For green coffees and equipment for home roasting try *www.fantes.com* (800-878-5557) or *www. sweetmarias.com.* Home roasting has a particularly strong grassroots presence on the web. A search under "home coffee roasting" will net many additional useful sites.

Italian-style syrups for flavored espresso drinks can be difficult to turn up retail. Torani, the leading syrup manufacturer, supports an entertaining website at *www.torani.com* through which you can access retail sites that carry Torani products. DaVinci, which offers three lines of syrups, including a conventional line, an all-natural-ingredients line, and a sugar-free line, links visitors to retail sources for its syrups at *www.davincigourmet.com.* Both sites also supply recipes and other syrup-related information. The Monin site (*www.monin.com*) is impressive, but currently fails to provide links to retail sources for its syrups.

Three useful sites for purchasing chais: *www. chaistall.com* offers a very authentic chai; *www.buychai. com* carries a wide variety of nicely crafted if less authentic chais, and *www.chai-land.com* carries instant and commercial chais for those with no patience.

For purchasing equipment via the Internet, try *www.fantes.com,* or *www.sweetmarias.com.* Fante's also invites telephone orders (800-878-5557), and will research, find a source for, and special order any available piece of coffee equipment not currently in stock. Good cookware catalogs and sites also are useful, particularly Chef's Catalog (*www.chefscatalog.com,* 800-338-3232). Or try searching the Internet for the names of equipment manufacturers: searches for Saeco, Pavoni, Faema, Capresso, Rancilio, Gaggia, Braun, and Krups all will net useful sites. In most cases the companies maintain their own sites, but searching for the manufacturer name will provide a means of comparison shopping plus offer up occasional unexpected pleasures, like the delightful Pavoni enthusiasts' site *www.kazys.net.*

Finally, a more traditional source for high-end espresso gear, including exotic piston machines, is Thomas Cara (415-781-0383), an old San Francisco family business run by people who know the equipment they sell thoroughly and support it unstintingly. No website, just knowledgeable, friendly owners and a basement full of replacement parts.

Advice on Espresso as Business

Those readers contemplating entering the coffee or espresso business and who are seeking advice should plan to attend the annual meeting and show of the Specialty Coffee Association of America (562-624-4100; *www.scaa.org*), usually held in late April or early May. NASCOR, the North American Specialty Coffee & Beverage Retailers' Expo (800-548-0551; *www.freshcup.com/nascore*), hosts a somewhat smaller show in October. Coffee Fest (206-232-2982; *www.coffeefest.com*) holds shows at several locations across the country over the course of the year.

Although I can't imagine entering the business without attending at least one of these events, publications and video tapes are also helpful. For book-length publications and video tapes on the espresso business contact the Specialty Coffee Association of America fulfillment center (800-647-8292; *www.scaa.org*) or Bellissimo Coffee Education Group (800-655-3955; *www.espresso101.com*). Trade magazines include the widely read and influential *Tea & Coffee Trade Journal* (212-391-2060; *www.teaandcoffee.net*); the somewhat more espresso-oriented *Fresh Cup* (503-236-2587; *www.freshcup.com*); the *Specialty Coffee Retailer* (847-427-9512; *www.specialty-coffee.com*), and *Gourmet Retailer Magazine* (305-446-3388; *www.gourmetretailer.com*). In addition to the websites associated with these publications, *www.coffeeuniverse.com* and the Specialty Coffee Association of America site (*www.scaa.org*) are very helpful.

The Specialty Coffee Association of America offers an excellent series of espresso workshops and associated training opportunities. Two reliable espresso-business consultants are Bellissimo Coffee Education Group (800-655-3955; *ciao@teleport.com*) and Sherri Miller & Associates (303-863-0897; *millers40@aol.com*).

ILLUSTRATION SOURCE

Chapter Opening Illustrations

Preface, page vii: The excitement of early espresso culture captured in a 1922 Victoria Arduino poster: power, speed, sophistication, modernity; fast trains and espresso-powered people.

Chapter 1, page 1: This older Venetian coffee sign suggests that all of the imagined dark romance of Africa was available to those Italians of the period who chose to purchase a cup of Poggi coffee.

Chapter 2, page 9: A gondola-load of Victoria Arduino espresso machines ready for delivery in early twentieth-century Venice. The sheer quantity of shiny new machines in one place at one time suggests how rapidly espresso culture spread through Italy during the years preceding World War I.

Chapter 3, page 35: One of many witty celebrations of espresso culture currently decorating the torsos of North Americans. From a T-shirt design by Rebecca Lee Baldwin for Fabric Art, Inc., Portland, Oregon.

Chapter 4, page 49: An open-air coffee-roasting stand in early twentieth-century Spain, before ground canned coffees started the world on its steep slide to coffee mediocrity.

Chapter 5, page 59: Early eighteenth-century illustration of coffee branch, flowers, and fruit from Jean de La Roque's *Voyage de l'Arabie Heureuse.*

Chapter 6, page 79: On a Costa Rican coffee farm early in this century, water carries coffee fruit from fields to a central processing facility. This photograph gives a good notion of the relatively small scale of commercial *Coffea arabica* trees.

Chapter 7, page 93: This extraordinary device, designed by Mario Levi and first manufactured in 1919, combines roasting, grinding, and brewing processes in a single apparatus.

Chapter 8, page 108: This device from 1930s Italy woke its owner to a demitasse of freshly brewed espresso. At the appointed time the clock activated the electric element in the little caffettiera in the center of the device; when steam pressure in the caffettiera had forced enough fresh espresso into the cup at the right to trigger a balance mechanism, the alarm sounded.

Chapter 9, page 121: Two tapered streams of perfect crema.

Chapter 10, page 157: Tourists and accommodating waiter pose in front of Venice's Caffè Florian in the 1920s. The quintessence of touristic caffè glamour.

Photo and Illustration Credits

A'Roma Roasters & Coffee House, Santa Rosa, Calif., pages 53, 84.

Baldwin, Rebecca Less, illustration by Rebecca Baldwin for T-shirts and mugs by Fabric Art, Inc., Portland, Ore., page 35

BE-MA Editrice, Milan, Italy; Ambrogio Fumagalli's *Macchine da Caffè,* pages 13 (top), 24 (both), 25 (top), 26 (detail), 31 (both), 32 (top and center), 103

Brasilia s.r.l., Padua, Italy, and Rosito Bisani, Inc., Los Angeles, page 121

Braun, Inc., Lynnfield, Mass., pages 33 (bottom), 98, 149 (center)

Caffè Acorto Incorporated, Bellevue, Wash., page 27 (bottom)

Cimbali S.p.A., Milan, Italy, page 25 (bottom)

Davids, Kenneth, pages 1, 34 (top)

DeLonghi America, Carlstadt, N.J., page 116

FAEMA, S.p.A., Milan, Italy, and Gary Valenti, Inc., Maspeth, N.Y., page 26 (left)

Hulton Deutsch Collection, London, page 166

KRUPS North America, Inc., Closter, N.J., pages 115 (top), 149 (top)

Mosuki, Ltd./La Victoria Arduino, New York, pages vii, 9, 160

Nuova Simonelli, Belforte del Chienti, Italy, and Nuova Distribution Centre, Inc., Vancouver, B.C., Canada, page 27 (top)

Peerless Coffee Co., Oakland, Calif., George and Sonja Vukasin, owners, page 88

Pinacoteca di Brera, Milan, page 18

Robert Bosch Corporation, Broadview, Ill., page 99 (top)

Saeco U.S.A., Inc., Saddle Brook, N.J., page 33 (bottom), 100, 149 (bottom)

Tea & Coffee Trade Journal, New York: William Ukers' *All About Coffee,* pages 13 (bottom), 49, 55, 59, 62, 68, 79, 157, 161, 163, 169

Thomas Cara family collection, San Francisco, pages 32 (bottom), 33 (top)

UNIC S.A., Nice, France, page 93

Zassenhaus GmbH & co., Germany, and Windward Trading Co., San Rafael, Calif., page 99 (bottom)

INDEX